P9-DBT-282

ATLANTIS
FACT or FICTION?

ATLANTIS
FACT or FICTION?

Edited by

EDWIN S. RAMAGE

Contributors

J. Rufus Fears
S. Casey Fredericks
John V. Luce
Edwin S. Ramage
Dorothy B. Vitaliano
Herbert E. Wright, Jr.

Indiana University Press
Bloomington and London

MANUFACTURED IN THE UNITED STATES OF AMERICA

Library of Congress Cataloging in Publication Data
Main entry under title:

Atlantis, fact or fiction?

Bibliography
Includes index.
1. Atlantis—Addresses, essays, lectures. I. Ramage, Edwin, S., 1929- II. Fears, J. Rufus.
GN751.A8 398'.42 77-23624
ISBN 0-253-10482-3 2 3 4 5 82 81 80 79

To Sue
Lyndall
Betty Rose
Charlene
Charles
Rhea Jane

Contents

Illustrations

MAPS

FIGURES

Preface

This collection of essays developed out of a panel discussion, "Atlantis: Fact or Fiction?" sponsored by the Department of Classical Studies at Indiana University in April 1975. All the contributors participated on the panel with the exception of Herbert E. Wright, Jr., whose essay has been added to round out the present collection.

In view of the thousands of books that have been written on the subject, one may well wonder whether another is needed. Can anything new be said about Atlantis? Perhaps not. But the purpose of this collection is a little different. It is an attempt to gather authorities from a number of disciplines—from language, mythology, history and archaeology, and geology—to look at Atlantis, each from his or her own point of view. In a sense, this is a break with the past, since most experts in these areas have been reticent to write about Atlantis in any detail. They have viewed it as being largely an emotional issue, attracting dilettantes, sensationalists, and, to some extent, members of the "lunatic fringe."

Recent entries in the pulp paperback book race to find Atlantis under, on, or over our earth provide a case in point. These books appear under eye-catching titles and between cleverly designed covers, and though they profess to be authoritative and to present new ideas, they are full of errors and are largely taken up with perpetuating notions and theories long outdated. They trade on the sensational and mysterious, and their purveyors attempt to impress the reader with facts that are largely fantasy and with reasoning that is really insinuation. As they do this, these would-be-experts casually brush aside any authority who happens to get in their way. It is little wonder that people who might otherwise have something worthwhile to say on the subject have turned away from Atlantis with a knowing smile or a disgusted shrug.

But the simple fact that there has been and continues to be so much speculation about Atlantis shows clearly that even the better-reasoned approaches have not provided a satisfactory solution. Actually, there is no consensus even as to whether or not a problem exists. This suggests that the whole Atlantis issue needs reconsideration and reevaluation from new perspectives and that perhaps those who are specialists in the various disciplines of which Atlantis is a part should be given a chance to provide these new perspectives. The essays which follow are meant to serve as a beginning of such evaluation.

Not much needs to be said about mechanics. Each writer brings to this collection a thorough knowledge of Atlantis as it relates to his or her particular expertise, and each has been free to develop his or her own point of view. Since each essay is meant to stand both by itself and as part of the collection, there is some repetition of ideas and bibliography from piece to piece. Although the editing has been kept to a minimum, an attempt has been made to remove unnecessary overlap, and we hope that what repetition remains will not prove distracting to the reader.

The introductory essay contains a translation and paraphrase of the relevant passages of Plato, as well as background material for the other essays.

Bloomington, Indiana

EDWIN S. RAMAGE

Note on the Contributors

J. Rufus Fears

Associate Professor of History at Indiana University; Director of the Vergilian School at Cumae, Italy, summer 1975; Guggenheim Fellow 1976. He has published a number of articles on Greek and Roman history and numismatics and has written a book—*Princeps a Diis Electus: The Divine Election of the Emperor as a Political Idea at Rome* (Rome, 1977) (*Papers and Monographs of the American Academy in Rome*, Vol. 26).

S. Casey Fredericks

Associate Professor of Classical Studies at Indiana University. He has published many articles on Roman satire, mythology, and science fiction, as well as a book, *Roman Satirists and Their Satire* (Park Ridge, N.J., 1974) (with Ramage and Sigsbee).

John V. Luce

Associate Professor of Classics and Public Orator, Dublin University, Ireland. He specializes in Greek literature, philosophy, and culture, and has published extensively on Greek topics: *The End of Atlantis* (London and New York, 1969; U.S. title: *Lost Atlantis*); *The Quest for America* (London, 1972) (with others); *The Quest for Ulysses* (London, 1974) (with Stanford); *Homer and the Heroic Age* (London, 1975).

Edwin S. Ramage

Professor of Classical Studies at Indiana University. He has published articles on Latin literature and archaeology and the following books: *Urbanitas: Ancient Sophistication and Refinement* (Norman, Okla., 1973); *Roman Satirists and Their Satire* (Park Ridge, N.J., 1974) (with Fredericks and Sigsbee); translation of Ulrich Knoche, *Roman Satire* (Bloomington, Ind., 1975).

Dorothy B. Vitaliano

Geologist with the United States Geological Survey, specializing in volcanology and in the technical translation of foreign language material. She has published a number of articles on the eruption of Santorini: "Plinian Eruptions, Earthquakes, and Santorini—A Review," *Acta of the First International Scientific Congress on the Volcano of Thera, Greece, 1969* (Athens, 1971), 81–108 (with C. J. Vitaliano); "Volcanic Tephra on Crete," *American Journal of Archaeology* 78 (1974), 19–24 (with C. J. Vitaliano). She has also published a review essay on Atlantis in the *Journal of the Folklore Institute* 8 (1971), 68–76, and a book, *Legends of the Earth: Their Geologic Origins* (Bloomington, Ind., 1973) (nominated for the National Book Awards in the science category).

H. E. Wright, Jr.

Regents' Professor of Geology, Ecology, and Botany, Director of the Limnological Research Center, and Professor in the Center for Ancient Studies, University of Minnesota. He teaches glacial geology and Quaternary paleoecology and has participated in many archaeological projects in the Near East and in Greece, as well as in Peru and Labrador. Among the articles he has written that are relevant to the present book is "Tunnel Valleys, Glacial Surges, and the Subglacial Hydrology of the Superior Lobe in Minnesota," *Geological Society of America Memoir* 136 (1973), 251–76.

PERSPECTIVES ANCIENT AND MODERN

Perspectives Ancient and Modern

EDWIN S. RAMAGE

The philosopher Plato, writing in Athens a little more than 2,300 years ago, at two points in his dialogues gives a description of the rise and fall of what he calls "a power that insolently advanced against Europe and Asia together, mounting its attack from outside—from the Atlantic Ocean." He goes on to call this power "the island Atlantis," little realizing what a storm of interest and controversy his account was going to produce. In both ancient and modern times attitudes have ranged from unquestioning belief in the truth of what Plato says to frank rejection of the whole idea. The Greeks and Romans included Atlantis in their geographic speculations, and the early Christian Fathers found this mysterious island very useful for purposes of allegory. In modern times many occultists, mystics, and religious fanatics have chosen Atlantis as a base for their beliefs. Scientists and pseudoscientists have used Atlantis to create land bridges between Europe and America, to recreate the geological history of the Atlantic sea-bottom, and to prove connections between the early populations of the Americas and Europe. There is now even a new word, "Atlantologist," which has been coined to describe a person who has become an expert on matters involving Atlantis. And we should not forget

The Western Mediterranean, Italy, Spain, and North Africa, with Plato's Atlantis added.

the many Atlantises of the past, present, and future that have surfaced in science fiction literature.

All of this activity has a long history, extending from Plato's time to the present with only a single interruption. This was a period

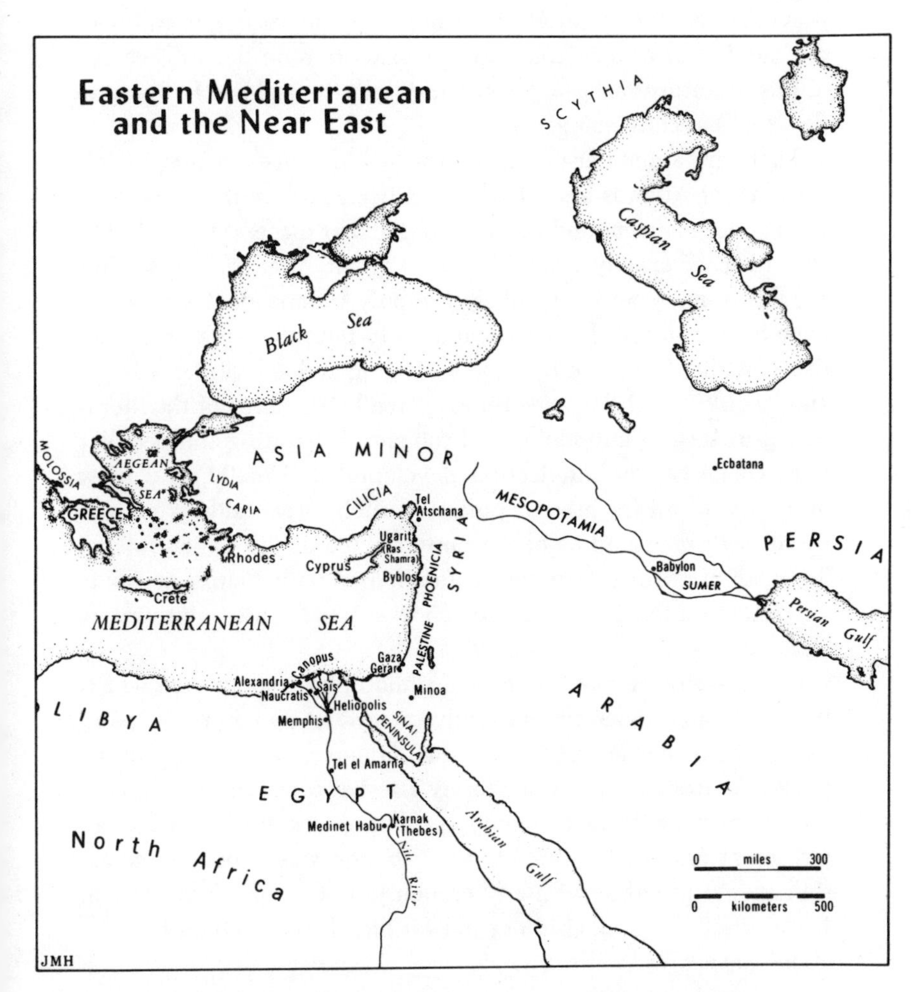

The Eastern Mediterranean, Greece, and the Near East.

between the sixth and eleventh centuries, during a large part of which intellectual activity in general was suspended. It is difficult to know how many books have been written about Atlantis over this long period of time. A reasonable round number seems to be 2,000, though estimates range as high as 10,000. Even at the lower figure we would have to read a book a day for the best part of six years to cover the material. It is completely impossible to estimate the number of articles that have been written on the subject. All of this literature makes a fascinating study in itself, as L. Sprague de Camp has convincingly shown.[1]

There are a number of reasons for looking once again at Plato's accounts of Atlantis and at what has been said on the subject by writers both ancient and modern. In the first place, it will serve to remind us of exactly what Plato said about Atlantis. He is, after all, the primary and very likely the only independent source we have for the story. This will enable us to put into proper perspective what has been said by way of locating and describing Atlantis and its culture. At the same time, even a brief survey of the literature provides a glimpse of one of the most interesting and peculiar phenomena of our intellectual development. Finally, and most important of all for present purposes, such a reconsideration and survey will be useful as background for the essays which follow, for most of them presuppose a familiarity with Plato's accounts and at least a passing acquaintance with what subsequent writers have said.

Plato's writings take the form of philosophic dialogues in which the philosopher Socrates is usually present as a main participant. But in the *Timaeus* and *Critias,* the dialogues in which Plato discusses Atlantis, he plays a largely passive role. The two pieces take their titles from the main speakers in each case and were written at roughly the same time. Although it is impossible to assign a date to either with any certainty, both come fairly late in Plato's life. It is probably not too far off, then, to assign them to about 350 B.C.

The Tale of Atlantis in the Timaeus

Plato makes it clear at the beginning of the *Timaeus* that this dialogue is meant to follow the *Republic* as a kind of sequel, while the tale of Atlantis provides clear connection between the *Timaeus* and the *Critias.* In the *Republic* Plato has provided a picture of his ideal state with its government, social structure, and system of education. In the *Timaeus,* which falls dramatically on the day after the *Republic,* the philosopher gives an account of the creation of the universe down to the creation of man, with Timaeus developing the argument and Socrates, Critias, and Hermocrates participating as listeners and to some extent as commentators.

But before the main discussion begins, Socrates summarizes in an informal way what has been said about the ideal state in the *Republic* (*Timaeus* 17a–20c). When he has finished, Hermocrates mentions the fact that after the previous day's discussion Critias had told a story from some time past which bore on the subject, and he asks his friend to tell it again. Here is Critias' story, then, with Socrates, Timaeus, and Hermocrates listening (*Timaeus* 20d–25e).

CRITIAS: All right, then, Socrates, listen to a story that is very strange, but one that is in every respect true, as Solon, the wisest of the seven wise men, once asserted. For you see he was a relative and close friend of my great-grandfather Dropides, as he himself frequently points out in his poetry. And Dropides told Critias, my grandfather, and he in turn told us when he was an old man that there were great and amazing exploits of this city of ours in earlier times which had disappeared with the lapse of years and the passing of men. And it would be quite proper for us to recall the greatest of these actions both to pay you back a favor and at the same time to honor the goddess fairly and honestly at her festival with a story like this.

SOCRATES: Well put. But what is this action that Critias recounted as not being mere hearsay but something actually done by this city in early times on the evidence of Solon?

CRITIAS: I will tell you; it is an old story I heard from a man no longer young. For at that time Critias, as he admitted himself, was already pretty close to ninety years old, while I was about ten at the most. It happened to be Children's Day for us at the Apaturia.[2] The boys were going through the usual routine at the festival, when our fathers gave us prizes for reciting poetry. Many poems by many poets were recited and quite a number of us boys read those of Solon because they were new at that time. And so one of the members of our tribe—either he really thought so at that time or else he was conveying a compliment to Critias—said it seemed to him that just as Solon was the wisest of men in other respects, so in poetry he was also the noblest of all the poets.

Then the old man—for I remember the situation very well—was quite pleased and smiled as he said: "If only he had not treated poetry as an avocation, Amynander, but had pursued it as others did and completed the story which he brought back here from Egypt. Instead, he had to put it aside because of the unrest and other problems which he found when he arrived home. In my opinion, at any rate, neither Hesiod nor Homer nor any other poet would ever have had a better reputation than he."

"And what was the story, Critias?" asked the other.

"It involves a very great exploit and one that could with complete justification be called the most glorious action of all those undertaken by this city, though the story of it has not survived to the present because of the passing of time and because those who did it have died."

"Tell us from the beginning, then, what Solon said and what the circumstances were, and do tell us also from whom he heard it as being the truth."

"In Egypt, in the delta," the other went on, "where the river Nile divides at its mouth, there is the Saïtic district. The largest city here is Saïs where in fact Amasis was king. There is a certain founding goddess of their city whose name is Neïth in Egyptian, and in Greek, according to what they say, it is Athena. They say they have a special affection for Athens and that to a certain degree they are related to the people here. Indeed, Solon said that when he arrived there he was greatly honored by the Egyptians, and when he was inquiring about past history of those of the priests who were expert in these matters, he found that hardly any Greek—neither he nor anyone else—knew anything, so to speak, about such things. And at one point, when he wanted to draw them into a discussion of ancient history, he attempted to speak about the oldest traditions here—to tell the myth of Phoroneus, who is said to have been the first man, and Niobe and again to tell the story of Deucalion and Pyrrha after the flood and how they survived. He also gave the genealogy of their descendants, and by enumerating the years that had elapsed since the events that he was describing he tried to compute the dates. And one of the priests who was extremely old said 'Oh Solon, Solon, you Greeks are always children; there is no such thing as an old Greek.' And hearing this, Solon said, 'And what do you mean by this?' 'All of you,' he replied, 'are young in knowledge and experience. For in your minds you have not a single idea that is ancient according to any time-honored tradition or any kind of learning that is gray with age. And there is a reason for this. There have been and will be many different destructions of mankind. The greatest are by fire and water, but there are other lesser destructions caused by thousands of other agencies.

" 'For there is a tale told among you also that once upon a time Phaethon, the son of Helios, harnessed his father's chariot and because he was unable to drive it along his father's road, he burned the things on the earth and perished himself after being struck by a thunderbolt. Now this tale as it is told has the appearance of a myth, but the truth of it lies in a movement of the bodies in the sky as they go around the world and in the destruction after long periods of time of things on earth in a great conflagration. At such a time, then, those who live in the mountains and in places that are high and dry die in greater numbers than those who live near the rivers and the sea. In our case the Nile, which is our savior in other respects as well, then too saves us from this difficulty by overflowing. On the other hand, when the gods inundate and cleanse the earth with water, the herdsmen and shepherds on the hills come through safely, while those living in your cities are swept away by the rivers into the sea. In this country, however, neither then nor at any other time does the water pour into our fields from above; quite to the contrary, it rises up naturally from below. And so it is for these reasons that the things preserved here are considered to be very ancient. The truth of the matter is that in all of the places where neither violent winter nor the scorching heat of summer prevents it people do exist, though in greater numbers at one time than at another.

" 'And whatever we learn about by report as happening among you or here or in some other place, whether it is something noble or great or stands out for some other reason, all of these things have been written down here from early times and preserved in our temples. But you and others as well happen to have been provided with writing only recently in each case along with all the other things that cities need. Then after the normal number of years the torrent from heaven comes bearing down like a plague and leaves only the unlettered and uneducated from among you alive. And so you become new people all over again, as it were, knowing nothing of what existed in ancient times either here or among your own people.

" 'Indeed, Solon, the pedigree-tracing which you went through just now relating to the people in your country differs little at all from children's fairy tales. For you remember just one destruction of the earth, though many happened earlier. And, what is more, you do not realize that the finest and noblest race among men once lived in your land and that you and your whole city are in a line from them—from a little seed that happened to survive. No, you have not learned about this because for many generations the survivors died without being able to put it into writing. And it is a fact, Solon, that at one time before the greatest deluge what is now the city of Athens was a leading military power and extremely well governed in all respects. It is said that her exploits and her constitution were the finest of all that we have heard about in the world.'

"Upon hearing this, Solon said that he was surprised and with all eagerness asked the priests to go through everything known about these early citizens in detail from beginning to end.

"Then the priest said: 'Yes, I will, Solon, and I will do this for you and for your city and above all for the goddess to whose lot both your city and this one fell and who nurtured and educated both—yours a thousand years earlier when she had received the seed of you from Earth and Hephaestus and this one later. And the length of time taken for our development here is given as 8,000 years in the sacred writings. As far as the citizens that lived 9,000 years ago are concerned, I will outline briefly some of their laws and describe their finest exploit. Later when we have the time we will go through everything in detail from beginning to end using the records themselves.

" 'Consider their laws, then, by looking at those here. For you will discover here and now many examples of those which existed in your state at that time. First of all, the priestly caste is set apart from the others; and then there is this classification of workers where each group works separately without mixing with another. This is also the case with the classes of herdsmen, hunters, and farmers. And what is more, you have perhaps noticed that the military class here is separated from all the other classes, for they are assigned to take care of nothing besides matters of warfare. Moreover, the kind of arms they use is the shield and spear which we were the first people of Asia to use for fighting after the goddess taught us to use them. Similarly in your part of the world she revealed this to you first. Again, as far as knowledge is concerned, you perhaps see the law here—how much care has been given right from the beginning to the nature of the universe and to discovering all things for human life that come from these divine principles. These extend right to divination and doctoring for good health and include the acquisition of all those other sciences that follow upon these.

" 'At that time, then, the goddess established you in a city before all others after providing you with all of this well-ordered system. And she chose the place where you were born because she saw that the well-balanced climate there would produce men of the greatest wisdom. Since she was herself a lover of war and wisdom, the goddess chose a place that would produce men most like her and located her first establishment there.

" 'And so you lived under laws like these and under even better laws, surpassing all men in every virtue, as was only right for those who had been produced and reared by the gods. Thus it is that there are many great actions of your city written down here that are marvelled at. And of all of these one stands out because of its magnitude and because of the courage it involved. For the records show how your city once stopped a great power as it was arrogantly spreading itself over the whole of Europe and Asia together, after starting from the Atlantic Ocean outside. For at that time the sea was navigable there, and there was an island in front of the mouth which you Greeks call the Pillars of Heracles [Strait of Gibraltar]. The island was larger than Libya and Asia taken together, and from it there was access to the other islands for those making the trip at that time. From these islands they could go right to the continent opposite, the one that encircles that real sea. For all of this that lies within the mouth which I am talking about seems to be a kind of harbor with a narrow entrance. But that outside is really an ocean and the land surrounding it may be quite correctly called a continent.

" 'Now on this island of Atlantis there arose a great and marvelous power with kings ruling over all the island, as well as many of the other islands and parts of the continent. What is more, of those lands here inside they ruled over Libya as far as Egypt and Europe as far as central Italy. At one point, then, this power, completely united, tried with one assault to enslave your country, our country, and all the territory within the strait. Then it was, Solon, that the power of your city stood out for all men because of the courage and strength that she showed. For she surpassed all in valor and expertise in war, serving on the one hand as the leader of the Greeks and on the other hand standing alone out of necessity when the others deserted her. After experiencing extreme danger, she defeated the invaders and set up a memorial to her victory. Thus she prevented those who had not yet been enslaved from being made slaves and ungrudgingly set free the others of us who live within the boundaries of Heracles.

" 'But at a later time there occurred violent earthquakes and floods and one terrible day and night came when your fighting force all at once vanished beneath the earth and the island of Atlantis in similar fashion disappeared beneath the sea. And for this reason even now the sea there has become unnavigable and unsearchable, blocked as it is by the mud shallows which the island produced as it sank.' "

Now you have heard, Socrates, in an abbreviated way what the elder Critias reported following the account of Solon. And when you were speaking yesterday about the state and the men you had in mind, I was amazed as I remembered these things that I have just told you and as I came to realize what a strange stroke of fate it was that your description in most respects agreed exactly with the story Solon told.

The Tale of Atlantis in the Critias

There is much more detail in the *Critias*, but the story remains incomplete because the piece breaks off abruptly in the middle of the narrative. There is no way of knowing the reason for this. It is possible that Plato tired of what he was writing or wrote himself into a corner and abandoned the project. It is equally possible that the last part of the dialogue has simply been lost.

Socrates, Timaeus, and Hermocrates are once again present as listeners, and after some introductory discussion Critias begins his story (108c–121c). It is too long to quote in its entirety here, so a summary will have to suffice. Key passages have, however, been translated, as the quotations below indicate.

Critias first makes the point that this story was told by the priests in Egypt to Solon, who brought it back to Greece (108d).

"And first of all," he goes on to say, "let us remember that the total length of time from when the war between those living outside beyond the Pillars of Heracles and all those living inside was reported as taking place was 9,000 years. This war I now have to discuss in detail. Athens, then, was described as leading the one side and fighting through the whole war, while the kings of the island of Atlantis led the other side. I said that the latter was in fact an island that was at one time larger than Libya and Asia, though it now has been sunk by earthquakes and has produced a barrier of impassable mud so that those sailing from here toward the open sea can no longer make headway" (108e–109a).

Critias now describes how the gods divided up the earth with each receiving his or her fair share and how they guided the humans who grew up in each state. Hephaestus and Athena took Athens and established men of enlightenment and courage here. "And the names of these citizens have been preserved, while their exploits have disappeared because of the dying off of those who succeeded them and because of the long passage of time. For, as was said before, the survivors on each occasion were illiterate mountain men who had heard only the names of the rulers in this land and knew little more of their exploits." As proof of the fact that names have been preserved, Critias points to Solon's statement that the Egyptian priests when describing this early war mentioned a number of Greek names (109b–110c).

In the early period there existed in Athens all the various classes of citizens and especially the military caste, which had been separated from the others. This group was state-supported, possessed no private property, received only enough resources to support their existence, and carried out all the duties of the guardians mentioned in the *Republic*. Attica in those days had a great deal of fertile land which supplied everything in abundance. But "many great floods in the 9,000 years—for this is the number of years that have passed from that time to the present—" had caused much of it to erode away and disappear into the sea. In Critias' time, then, it was not as rich as it had been in those earlier days when the farmer did his cultivating expertly and was aided by an abundant supply of water and an ideal climate (110c–111e).

The Acropolis used to be much larger and in the early period was covered with arable land. While the craftsmen of the city lived beneath it, the military class alone had the right to live on the Acropolis itself. Here they had their community dwellings and mess hall. And they made certain that their numbers stayed close to 20,000. The Athenians living this ideal life in ideal circumstances had gained a reputation throughout Europe for their handsome appearance and high moral character (112a–112e).

At this point Critias turns to describe Atlantis, but as he does so he seeks to forestall any confusion that his listeners may feel at hearing Greek names connected with Atlantis: "Solon," he says, "intended to make use of the story for his poetry, and as he was searching out the meaning of the names, he found that the Egyptians who were the first to write them down had brought them over into their own tongue. He in turn determined the meaning of each name, translated it into our language, and wrote it down. And these writings were in my grandfather's possession and now belong to me, and I learned them thoroughly when I was a child" (113a–113b).

And so he begins his description of Atlantis. At the allotment of the lands of the earth mentioned earlier, Poseidon took the island of Atlantis as his share. He had ten sons, five pairs of twins, for whom he divided the island into ten parts. The oldest received the largest and most fertile part, which lay in a large plain running through the center of the island, and he was to be the dominant ruler. This king was called Atlas after the island and the Atlantic Ocean. Critias also provides the names of all the other sons and mentions the fact that together they extended their power over many other islands in the ocean and as far east as Egypt and central Italy (113b–114c).

Atlas was succeeded in the kingship by a long line of descendants and Atlantis became the wealthiest city that had ever existed. She not only imported many commodities, but she also produced most of the everyday necessities of life herself. The list is extensive: metals of all kinds (including orichalcum, which was perhaps an alloy of copper and second only to gold in value), wood for building, animals both tame and wild (including elephants), herbs, spices, liquid gums, grapes, grain, vegetables, and "the produce of trees." And the people who lived here built a complex and beautiful city with each king adding to the splendor. The city consisted of a central island, where the king lived in a fine palace, surrounded by three concentric circles of water alternating with two of land. The former were bridged to make a walkway, and a passageway was bored through the circles of land to provide ships access to the island in the center. From the outermost circle a channel was dug to the sea some distance away (figure 1).

The rings of land and the central island had walls around them with towers and gates at the appropriate places. The outermost wall was sheathed with bronze, the second with tin, and the one around the citadel itself with orichalcum. Within the citadel was a temple to Cleito and Poseidon with a wall of gold around it, and also a temple to Poseidon covered with silver except for the acroteria, which were gilded. The interior was decorated with gold, silver, ivory, and orichalcum and contained a greater than life size statue of Poseidon in his chariot, the whole thing made of gold. There were many other fine pieces as well. Critias says that the palace was fitted out in a similarly splendid manner (114c–117a).

The people enjoyed both hot and cold springs and made full use of them. Among other things, they had built baths for their kings and for their citizens, and even the beasts of burden had theirs. On the circles of land there were many temples, gardens, gymnasia, and exercising areas for horses. On the outermost circle was a large racecourse, and here also was stationed the larger part of the king's bodyguard. The more reliable of these were located on the innermost circle, while those who could be trusted without qualification had a place on the island itself. Finally, Critias tells us, the shipyards were full of warships and equipment for these. Encircling all of this was another wall about six miles further out which had houses built on it (117a-117e).

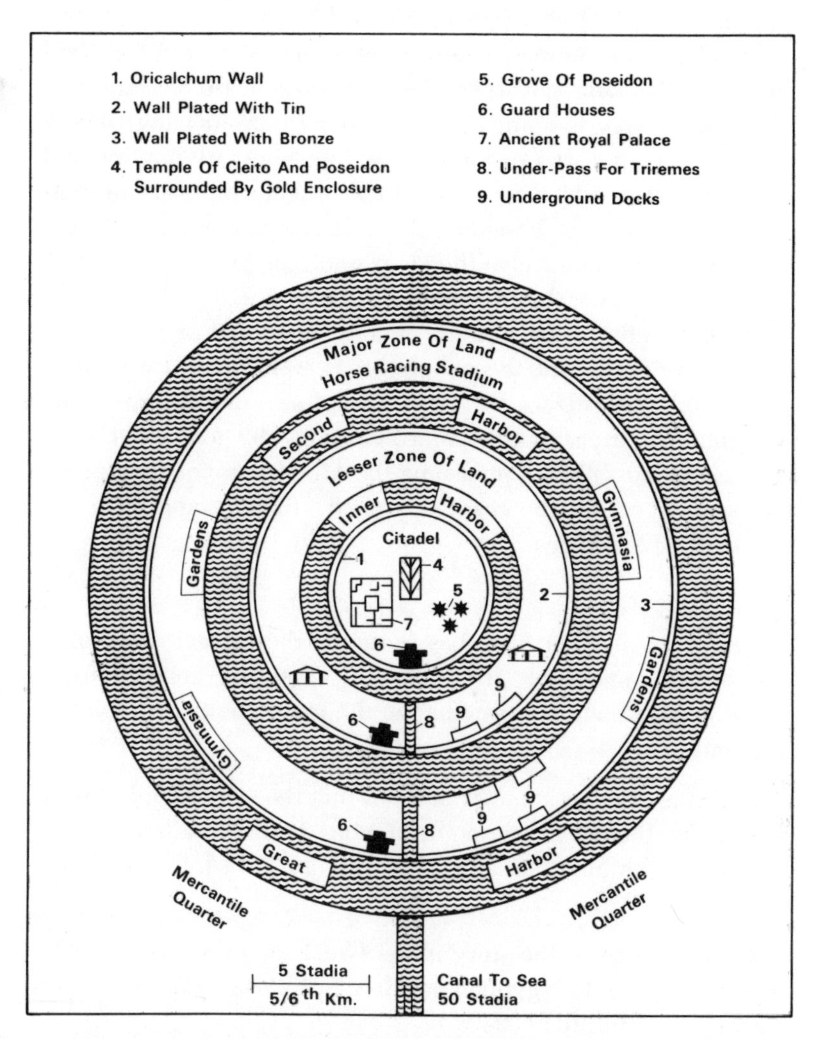

Figure 1. Plan of Plato's Atlantis, from J. V. Luce, *The End of Atlantis,* by permission of Thames and Hudson Ltd.

Critias now describes the country around the city (117e–118e) and then turns to discuss the way in which levies were made for war. He mentions horses and chariots, hoplites, archers, slingers, javelin-throwers, and sailors. There were 10,000 chariots in this force and some 1,200 warships (118e–119b).

The kings ruled autonomously in their own cities, but laws laid down by Poseidon governed their relations with one another. Alternately every five and every six years they met together to perform a complicated religious ritual involving bull hunting and sacrificing, after which they gave their judgments regarding possible transgression of Poseidon's laws. It is significant that all the laws Critias quotes involve the kings and their relationships with one another and not the citizens that they rule (119c–120d).

The last section of the *Critias* contains an account of the gradual moral deterioration of the people of Atlantis from law-abiding, gentle, virtuous citizens to a state of ugliness, unhappiness, and uncurbed ambition. At this point Zeus calls the gods together to discuss the possibility of punishing the Atlanteans, and he is about to speak when, to the reader's dismay, the dialogue abruptly breaks off (120d–121c).

Here, then, is what Plato has to say on the subject of Atlantis, and before going on to the views of succeeding generations, it might be worthwhile to summarize the main points of these two accounts:

1. Critias insists a number of times that the story he is telling is a true one, though at one point (*Critias* 107b) he admits that it can only be an imitation and representation, which for Plato was twice removed from reality.

2. The source of the story is the Greek statesman Solon, who received it from the Egyptian priests at Saïs. (He was evidently on his travels a little after 600 B.C.).

3. The story takes place 9,000 years before Solon's time, though there is a discrepancy here. In the *Timaeus* this is the date of the founding of Athens, while in the *Critias* it is the time of war between Athens and Atlantis.

4. Athens is a flourishing city organized along the lines of Plato's ideal city as it is described in the *Republic.*

5. Atlantis is a large island in the Atlantic Ocean just outside the Pillars of Heracles or what we now call the Strait of Gibraltar. There are other islands beyond, from which there is access to "the mainland" some distance away.

6. Atlantis is ruled by kings, with the largest and most flourishing city serving as leader.

7. At the time of the war with Athens, Atlantis had extended her power as far as Egypt on the south and central Italy on the north.

8. Sometime after the Athenians had defeated the Atlanteans, both powers were the victims of earthquakes and floods and both disappeared in the space of a day and a night.

9. The Atlantic Ocean is unnavigable where Atlantis previously existed because of residual mud from the sinking of the island.

This is perhaps not the place to editorialize at length on the reliability of Plato's account, but a few comments are necessary to offset misconceptions that keep appearing in the Atlantis literature. In the first place, although the evidence is sparse, archaeology has shown that the Athens which Plato describes could not have existed in 9500 B.C. or thereabouts. At that time Greece was in the late Palaeolithic period and man was still living in caves or rock shelters and was hunting and gathering his food. Settlement was not to begin for another 3,000 years, and even then the process of civilization was a slow one.[3] No amount of rationalizing can produce Plato's well-governed, well-structured, and well-protected state in this early period.

If we accept the date as being what Plato wrote—and there is no good reason for rejecting or changing it—we have to assume that it fits with the philosopher's purposes. Plato makes the point a number of times that this early Athenian state was in most, if not all, respects identical with the ideal state which he described in the *Republic.* But from what we know about Athens and its history, this particular combination of political, social, and military elements did not exist at any time, neither in Mycenaean, nor in geometric, archaic, or classical Athens. What Plato seems to be doing with the *Timaeus* and *Critias*, then, is putting some of his theorizing of the *Republic* on a more practical level by giving an example of how it might work in practice. This is why Plato emphasizes the similarity between what has been described in the *Republic* and what Critias knows. And it is important that in the *Republic* it is Socrates who carries the theoretical discussion, while in the *Timaeus* and *Critias* it is Critias who confirms the theory by offering a practical example that just happens to have occurred to him. As Plato adapts Athenian history for his own purposes, he projects it into what for his Athenian listener was a thoroughly dim and dark past where it might become more believable.

More needs to be done with Athens' part in this whole Atlantis episode, though this is certainly not the place for it. People writing about Atlantis have for the most part ignored Athens, in spite of the fact that this city is the hero of the piece and it is the Athenian constitution and social structure that reflect Plato's ideals as they are developed in the *Republic.* But even a quick glance at what the philosopher says about Atlantis' protagonist suggests that he is not dealing with a historical situation, and this carries implications for the rest of his account, including the question of whether Atlantis ever existed.

The Ancient Perspective

The ancients' knowledge of geography was not nearly as extensive as ours is today, and this must be kept in mind by anyone reading Plato's account of Atlantis. Since the time of Homer in the seventh century B.C. the Greeks had considered all of the known world, which roughly included Europe, the Near East, and North

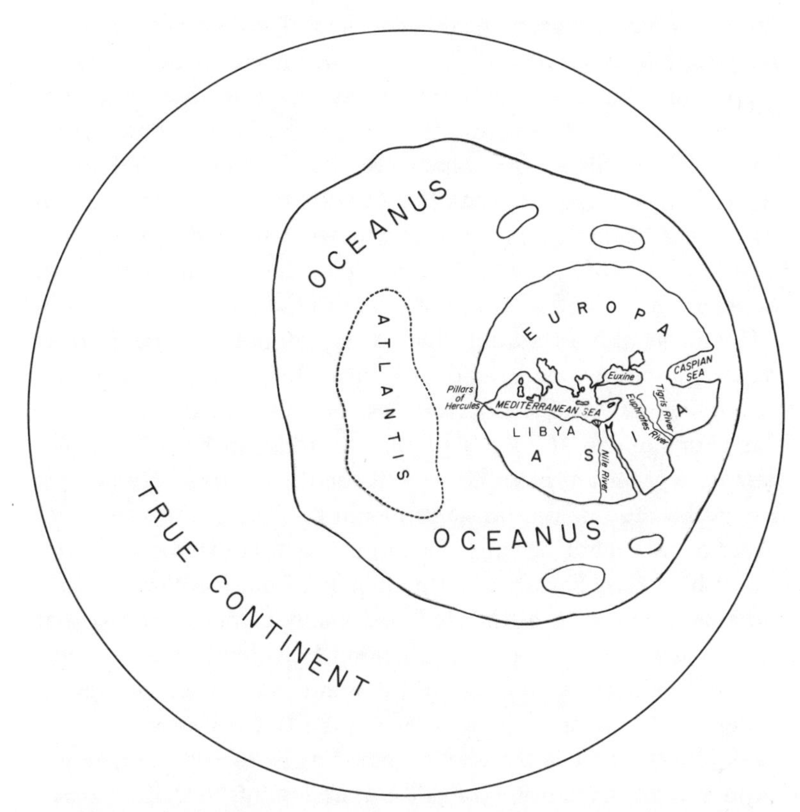

Figure 2. The known world according to the ancients, from D. B. Vitaliano, *Legends of the Earth,* by permission of Indiana University Press.

Africa, as being an island centered around a large lake which was actually the Mediterranean Sea. Around this island in turn ran a continuous river called Oceanus, or Ocean, on the other side of which was the "mainland" or "continent" (figure 2). This is not to say, however, that the ancients had ever seen North or South America, though some of the more venturesome—the Carthaginians, for example—had made their way into the Atlantic and had sailed down the coast of Africa and up the coast of Europe as far as Britain.

For the most part, however, the Atlantic Ocean beyond Gibraltar was a complete mystery to the ancients. The historian Tacitus, writing as late as A.D. 98, calls it "the unknown sea,"[4] while Plutarch in the same century is still convinced that the mysterious and magical island of Ogygia and the Isles of the Blest, where everything is a paradise, exist somewhere out beyond the Pillars of Heracles in what we now call the Atlantic Ocean.[5] This tradition had a long history going back to Homer, who had Odysseus in Book 11 of the *Odyssey* sail out into Oceanus where he summoned friends from the underworld to speak to him.

There was also a tradition that to venture out into the Atlantic was dangerous. A traveler of the fourth century B.C. says that if you sail out beyond the Pillars of Heracles you will run into great reefs.[6] The most famous of Plato's pupils, Aristotle, in his treatise *On Meteorology* tells of how the sea outside the Pillars of Heracles is shallow because of the presence of mud.[7] This reminds us of an earlier remark made by the fifth-century historian Herodotus, who tells of how King Sesostris of Egypt sailed from the Arabian Gulf and along the shores of the Red Sea, finally coming to a sea that was not navigable because of shallows.[8] Evidently these beliefs were still held by some people a thousand years later, for a geographer of the fourth century after Christ, Rufus Festus Avienus, speaks of the water in the western ocean as being extremely dense because of great quantities of salt in it and points to shallows, seaweeds, and sea monsters as making up some of the dangers that sailors must face out there.[9] This is the atmosphere, then, into which Plato was projecting his Atlantis, and this must be kept in mind when we consider Plato's account and what the ancient writers said about it.

Apparently Plato's story of Atlantis did not make the impression on the ancients that it has made on us. There are no treatises, long or short, on Atlantis. It is true that they may have existed, but if they did, they have vanished without a trace. For the most part we are dependent on random references in ancient writers, and it is perfectly clear that these are not always reliable. There is also an extensive commentary on the *Timaeus* and other dialogues written by Proclus, the Neoplatonist living in the fifth century after Christ. His work must be used with caution, however, since he wrote almost eight hundred years after Plato and was strongly under the influence of his mystical philosophy.

Evidently the controversy over Atlantis began as early as the generation after Plato, for his pupil Aristotle seems to have rejected Atlantis, while Crantor (approximately 335–275 B.C.), who was the first to write a commentary on the dialogues, accepted the story without qualification. According to Strabo, the famous geographer living in the time of Christ, Aristotle thought that the story was invented by Plato and that the destruction of the island by earthquake and flood was simply the philosopher's way of removing it from the stage.[10] Proclus writes of Crantor: "Some say that this whole story about the Atlanteans is straight history, as, for example, Crantor the first commentator on Plato."[11]

The next reference to Atlantis falls at least two centuries later, when Rome was well on her way to power in the Mediterranean. Once again Strabo provides the information. While discussing the settling of the earth through earthquakes and other means, the philosopher Posidonius, who was also Strabo's teacher, used Plato's story of Atlantis to make his point. Strabo cannot resist an editorial comment showing where he himself stands on the matter, for he says that Posidonius "does well to provide the statement of Plato as an example." After pointing to the fact that Plato has Solon report the existence and demise of Atlantis on the authority of the Egyptian priests, the geographer goes on: "And Posidonius thinks it is better to say this than that 'the one who made it obliterated it, as the poet did with the wall of the Achaeans.' "[12] Posidonius seems to have explicitly rejected Aristotle's position, since the quotation within the quotation here is generally taken as part of Aristotle's skeptical statement about Atlantis. Once again, then, we are given a glimpse of the controversy that must have been going on.

The next mention of Atlantis occurs in the *Natural History* of the polymath Pliny the Elder, who was writing in A.D. 77. When Pliny describes the formation of the Atlantic, he speaks of a great area of land being completely swept away "where the Atlantic Ocean is now—if we believe Plato."[13] Once again it is clear that disagreement about Atlantis exists. It is interesting to notice, however, that though Pliny feels he has to add a proviso, the story has become so much a part of scientific belief that it cannot be ignored.

At about the same time that Pliny wrote, Philo Judaeus, a Jewish philosopher whose works were destined to have great influence on subsequent Jewish and Christian writers, was putting together his writing based on the laws of Moses. In his treatise *On the Eternity of the World,* he raises the point that land is often swallowed up by the sea, and he includes among his examples "the island of Atalantes." He himself says that he is following Plato's account, and in relatively few words he shows this to be true when he describes the island as being greater than Africa and Asia and points to the fact that it was destroyed in a day and a night by earthquake and flood. He even asserts that the sea as a result was "full of abysses."[14] There can be no doubt that Philo accepts Plato's story at face value.

In the meantime, however, a new and interesting point of view was developing. By the time of Christ, Atlantis, in some men's minds at any rate, had taken its place beside the Isles of the Blest, the Hesperides, and Ogygia as part of the lore and mystery of Oceanus, which lay beyond the Pillars of Heracles. Somewhere around 30 B.C. Diodorus Siculus finished his *World History* in forty books. In the third book he deals with North Africa and as he does so he mixes together Amazons, Gorgons, and Atlanteans.[15] By now the Atlanteans have become highly civilized people living on the coast of Oceanus whom the Amazons defeat in battle. Here, Diodorus tells us, the gods were born, and with this he immediately launches into an extended discussion of the Atlanteans' ideas about the genesis of the gods. For Diodorus, then, it is no longer a case of whether Atlantis ever existed or not, but of how to relate its inhabitants to the other mythological peoples that lived out here at the end of the world. Most of what Diodorus says has to be taken as sheer embroidery.

We can see the same process of elaboration at work in Plutarch's

Life of Solon, which was written a little over a century later. By now the anonymous priest of Saïs has a name, Sonchis, and Solon is described as studying with him at Saïs and with Psenophis at Heliopolis. Plutarch goes on: "And hearing from them, as Plato says, the story of Atlantis, he tried to introduce it in a poem to the Greeks."[16] A little later Plutarch asserts that Solon began a great work on "the story or fable of Atlantis" but gave up, not because he could not find the time, as Plato says, but because his advanced age precluded his beginning the task. It is worth noting not only that Plato's story is in the process of elaboration here, but also that in Plutarch's eyes the tale of Atlantis has become either a story (*logon*) or a fable (*muthon*). The question of credibility is tied up in these two words, and it almost looks as if Plutarch is unwilling to commit himself.

There is enough mention of Atlantis in the third, fourth, and fifth centuries after Christ to show that it remained about as popular as before. Tertullian refers to it twice as an island that was lost beneath the Atlantic Ocean and in one of the two instances attributes the story to Plato.[17] Athenaeus, who was active about two hundred years after Christ, quotes a passage from Plato's account of Atlantis to illustrate the use of a word.[18] About the same time, the writer Aelian, who was an interesting combination of moralizer, anecdotist, and philosopher, tells the strange story of how the old kings of Atlantis are said to have worn the headband from a male sea-ram, and their queens the curls of its female counterpart.[19]

In the next century, Ammianus Marcellinus, who might be called the last great Roman historian, at one point in his *Roman History* talks about different kinds of earthquakes. As he describes the chasmatiae or "gaping" type, he points to the fact that these swallow up parts of the earth, "as in the Atlantic Ocean an island larger than all of Europe [was swallowed up]."[20] Once again, there is no indication of any skepticism about the truth of the story on Ammianus' part.

Proclus has already been mentioned as producing a commentary on the *Timaeus* in the fifth century after Christ. Although he is not the most reliable commentator we have, he has preserved some interesting material that shows to what extremes people had gone by his time in interpreting the story of Atlantis. Marcellus, a historian who wrote a history of the Ethiopians, tells of how the inhabitants of other islands in the Atlantic retain memories of the great and powerful island of Atlantis that used to exist there.[21] Proclus also mentions various allegorical interpretations. Amelius (third century after Christ) saw an analogy with the stars and planets in which Athens represented the stars, and Atlantis, with its seven circles, stood for the seven planets that were known at the time. At about the same time, Origen interpreted the war as a conflict between demons, some good and some bad, while a century earlier Numenius had taken the story as representing a conflict of souls. Porphyry too attempted an allegorical interpretation.[22]

And Proclus shows that the controversy over whether the tale is fact or fancy is still going on. Iamblichus, in the fourth century, and Proclus' teacher Syrianus were certain that the story was factual, while Longinus, Origen, and Numenius took the opposite point of view. Proclus himself, being a partisan of Plato, is a believer in Atlantis, although he would not go as far as Crantor and consider the account to be "straight history."[23]

It was Cosmas Indicopleustes, a traveler turned geographer, who had the last word on Atlantis as far as the ancient world is concerned. In his *Christian Topography,* which he wrote with the primary purpose of providing a Christian interpretation of geography to offset pagan ideas, he rejects the story out of hand, suggesting, as Aristotle had earlier, that destroying the island was a convenient way of ending the fiction.[24] But he leaves the reader less than confident in his critical ability, since in his version Timaeus tells the story, Solomon replaces Solon, much of the story comes from Moses, and God is responsible for sinking Atlantis.

As we look back over the ancient references, then, we catch a glimpse of the controversy over Atlantis that began shortly after Plato wrote and extended down to the end of antiquity. It is perhaps worth making the point once again, however, that there is no indication of an intense and sustained interest in Atlantis such as has been shown in modern times. Those who claim that many, or for that matter any, writings on Atlantis have been lost are simply speculating. There is nothing to show that this is so, and the burden lies with them to prove it.

It should also be noticed that most of the ancient writers who mention Atlantis have Plato's account in mind. Some mention the philosopher by name, others quote from him, and still others describe Atlantis in terms that are suspiciously close to what Plato says. In fact, everything points to Plato's *Timaeus* and *Critias* as being the only independent sources for the Atlantis story known to the ancients.

The Modern Perspective

To follow all the twists and turns of what may loosely be called Atlantis "scholarship" since the fifteenth century is all but impossible. Literally hundreds of people from every walk of life have contributed to the continuing saga—geographers, geologists, archaeologists, philologists, philosophers, novelists, poets, occultists, dilettantes, among others. Not only does the literature on Atlantis provide interesting insights into the history of human thought for the last five centuries or so, but it also serves as commentary on the nature of the human beast. The mystery of the unknown is always attractive, but in the case of Atlantis it has been especially tantalizing—so much so, in fact, that the whole issue at times has been as much a matter of emotion as it has of reason. Empty theory, dogmatic opinion, emotional prophecy, and blind belief, all elaborately expressed, have in nearly every generation taken their place beside well-weighed reason in attempts to explain the mysteries of Atlantis. To put it bluntly, a great deal of what has been written on the subject is useless and serves only to show how naïve and credulous people can be when writing or reading about Atlantis.

The controversy that we have traced from the generation after Plato down to late Roman times has continued right to the present. Each generation has had its believers and skeptics of every degree. The believers, however, tend to overshadow the skeptics for the simple reason that a positive theory, whether it is simple or elaborate, tends to be more attractive and to make better reading than any attempt at refutation, no matter how well taken it may be. Besides, the romantic side of man's nature leaves him naturally prejudiced in favor of the believer. We should remember, then, that while the pro-Atlantists probably outnumber the anti-Atlantists at any given time, the nonbelievers are always present with arguments that they feel disprove the existence of Atlantis, refute theory current or past, or offer reasonable rationalization of all or part of Plato's story.

When Atlantis makes its reappearance in literature, it is still connected with the Atlantic Ocean, which remains the mysterious, forbidding, and yet so very attractive stretch of water lying just beyond the edge of the known world. By the time Columbus was ready to make his voyage late in the fifteenth century, all kinds of strange and mythical islands had sprung up in the Atlantic to be added to those of antiquity. Somewhere to the west lay that island paradise, Avalon, to which, according to Geoffrey of Monmouth, King Arthur was taken to recuperate after being seriously wounded. Again, the Irish monk Saint Brendan, according to legend, had sailed the western sea looking for an earthly paradise. And he found it after many fabulous adventures with demons, sea serpents, and the like. The Isles of the Blest of Saint Brendan, which appear on maps as early as the thirteenth century, suggest an extension and adaptation of the ancient tradition which placed the Isles of the Blest in Oceanus beyond the Pillars of Heracles. Moreover, Atlantis itself must have been in the thoughts of some of the scholars of the time, for it appears on at least one fifteenth-century map.[25]

But with the discovery of the New World there came renewed

interest in the Atlantic, its islands, and the lands beyond. The sixteenth century brought the beginning of the intense search for Atlantis that has lasted to the present. Any division is arbitrary, but writing on Atlantis really falls into two periods—before and after 1882—for in this year Ignatius Donnelly published his *Atlantis: The Antediluvian World,* a book which had a strong influence on the Atlantis literature that followed.

During the period extending from the sixteenth through the nineteenth centuries, many theories and many attitudes were spawned—too many of them to discuss in any detail. But even a brief glance shows that speculation about Atlantis covered a wide spectrum. In all of these centuries there were scholars who either ignored Atlantis or explicitly rejected it. Another group allegorized and rationalized Plato's account. Some saw the deities which divided up the world as the personification of cosmological elements, while others equated the ten kings of Atlantis to ten great antediluvian epochs. The Bible also had its influence, not only as far as the location of Atlantis was concerned, as we shall see, but in other ways as well. The twelve tribes of Israel, for example, were equated with the ten kings of Atlantis and their cities.[26]

One of the most interesting interpretations was that of Bartoli, who in the eighteenth century saw behind the Athens-Atlantis conflict the real conflict between Athens and Persia which had erupted early in the fifth century B.C. The Athenians at this time had led the Greeks in successfully repelling the barbarian invasion. The parallels are quite striking, and Bartoli's explanation still finds acceptance in some quarters today.

But most of those who wrote about Atlantis in these centuries were more interested in locating it and identifying its remains if any were to be found. One school of thought subscribed to what might be called the debris theory. According to this, at least some of the islands scattered throughout the Atlantic were part of the debris left by the sudden and violent disappearance of Atlantis. The Madeiras, the Canaries, and the Azores were first taken as the remnants, but various theories soon included combinations of islands stretching all the way from Ireland in the Atlantic to the islands of the South Seas in the Pacific and even to New Zealand. America, too, became part of the puzzle, and one reconstruction showed Atlantis all but touching Africa on the east and America on the west, thus providing free passage from the Old World to the New for peoples wishing to populate America.

But one of the most popular ideas was that of Atlantis-in-America. And perhaps it was only natural that Atlantis should be identified with the newly discovered land to the west. The Spaniard Francesco López de Gómara first made the suggestion in 1553 and the idea was popular for the next three centuries. Quite a number of maps of the seventeenth and eighteenth centuries make the identification, and Sir Francis Bacon adopted it in his utopian novel *The New Atlantis.* It had a long run until about the middle of the nineteenth century, when it seems to have fallen out of favor, probably because increased knowledge of North America and of the ancient civilizations in Europe made the Old World–New World connections on which it was based pretty well untenable. It is interesting to notice, however, that the idea is brought up now and again even today.

While America had its proponents, many other parts of the world were chosen as sites for Atlantis. In fact, as man's knowledge increased, his imagination became ever more fertile and Plato's island took many forms. It was only natural, in view of the fact that some of the ancients had placed the Atlanteans in the far western part of Africa, that they should now be discovered there once again. Again, in the sixteenth century Serranus turned to the Bible for help, working along the same lines as Cosmas had earlier, to interpret Atlantis in terms of Mosaic law. The next logical step was to place Atlantis in Palestine, and early in the next century this interpretation was put forward. A little later, in 1762, Frederick Baër presented a detailed rationalization of Plato's account by which Atlantis became Judaea, the ten kingdoms there were somehow equated to the twelve tribes of Israel, the Atlantic Ocean became the Red Sea, and the sons of Atlas turned into the Israelites.

But the Bible was not the only guide used by Atlantis seekers. The seventeenth-century Swedish scholar Olaüs Rudbeck took the *Edda* in hand and discovered Atlantis in Sweden with its capital not far from Uppsala. In fact, Rudbeck found in Scandinavia the origins of all the peoples of Europe and Asia and the source of all their primitive ideas and traditions. His theories seem to have had considerable influence in his own time, and even today the idea of a Scandinavian Atlantis has its adherents.

One of the most elaborate and at the same time least original of the theories in these years was that of the eighteenth-century French astronomer Jean Bailly, who played the eclectic and adopted a number of ideas from his predecessors, including Rudbeck. Putting these ideas together and mixing in a large measure of imagination and speculation, Bailly placed Atlantis, that fine, fertile country mentioned by Plato, in the primitive glacial sea just off Spitsbergen. Using references culled from eastern writings, he showed how the Atlanteans advanced across Tartary, China, and Persia to Phoenicia and the shores of the Mediterranean. Atlas, according to him, was a king of Spitsbergen, a great astronomer, and a great thinker and inventor. Bailly was rather soundly refuted by his contemporaries, although some of those criticizing him invented theories that were about as unscientific, untenable, and just plain preposterous as Bailly's had been.

By now it is perhaps unnecessary to go on, except to point out that by the late nineteenth century the Atlanteans had also been connected with people as widely different in race and time as the Goths, the Gauls, the Druids, the Egyptians, and the Scyths and had been discovered in many other parts of the world: the Mediterranean, the Sahara, the Caucasus, in South Africa, Ceylon, Brazil, Greenland, the British Isles, the Netherlands, and Prussia.[27] At this point it might be well to remind ourselves of what Plato actually says about Atlantis. While his story leaves much room for interpretation, it hardly allows the license of moving it at will from one end of the world to the other.

We should not leave this earlier period of writing on Atlantis without some mention of perhaps the most eloquent refutation of Atlantis that has yet been put forward. In 1841 Henri Martin published his important commentary on the *Timaeus* in which he dealt at length with various aspects and problems of the dialogue.[28] After a thorough study of what Plato says, Martin makes seven points: (1) Plato's story is for all intents and purposes pure fiction; (2) It has an Egyptian, not a Greek origin; (3) The priests made up this story involving the Greeks for their own political advantage; (4) If Atlantis did exist, it was in the Atlantic just outside the Strait of Gibraltar, thus making it impossible to put it in Africa, the seas to the north, America, or Palestine; (5) It is impossible to believe that the sudden disappearance of an island as large as Atlantis would not have affected geography, and yet "the fable of Atlantis" presupposes that Europe, Asia, and Africa were as they are today when the island was in existence; (6) There was no continent running along the edge of Oceanus over which the Atlanteans could have extended their power, and there are no shallows where the island used to be; (7) We had best stop looking for Atlantis; it is truly Utopia ("Noplace").[29]

The search for Atlantis, however, did not stop, but took on a new momentum and a new direction with the publication of Donnelly's book in 1882.[30] Donnelly was an interesting person. After studying law he went on to be a newspaper editor, the lieutenant-governor of Minnesota, and a member of Congress. He was an eager reader, and during his eight years in Washington he spent much time in the Library of Congress reading widely on many different subjects. Besides writing on Atlantis, he also attempted to show by using cryptography that it was not Shakespeare who wrote the plays that have come down under his name, but Sir Francis Bacon.

After his political defeat in 1870, he retired to write the first of a number of books—that on Atlantis. This was a great success, so much so that by 1949 it had appeared in some fifty printings. Donnelly summarizes his purposes at the beginning by listing what he calls "several distinct and novel propositions." There are thirteen of these:

1. That there once existed in the Atlantic Ocean, opposite the mouth of the Mediterranean Sea, a large island, which was the remnant of an Atlantic continent, and known to the ancient world as Atlantis.
2. That the description of this island given by Plato is not, as has been long supposed, fable, but veritable history.
3. That Atlantis was the region where man first rose from a state of barbarism to civilization.
4. That it became, in the course of ages, a populous and mighty nation, from whose overflowings the shores of the Gulf of Mexico, the Mississippi River, the Amazon, the Pacific coast of South America, the Mediterranean, the west coast of Europe and Africa, the Baltic, the Black Sea, and the Caspian were populated by civilized nations.
5. That it was the true Antediluvian world; the Garden of Eden; the Gardens of the Hesperides; the Elysian Fields; the Gardens of Alcinous; the Mesomphalos; the Olympos; the Asgard of the traditions of the ancient nations; representing a universal memory of a great land, where early mankind dwelt for ages in peace and happiness.
6. That the gods and goddesses of the ancient Greeks, the Phoenicians, the Hindoos, and the Scandinavians were simply the kings, queens, and heroes of Atlantis; and the acts attributed to them in mythology are a confused recollection of real historical events.
7. That the mythology of Egypt and Peru represented the original religion of Atlantis, which was sun-worship.
8. That the oldest colony formed by the Atlanteans was probably in Egypt, whose civilization was a reproduction of that of the Atlantic island.
9. That the implements of the "Bronze Age" of Europe were derived from Atlantis. The Atlanteans were also the first manufacturers of iron.
10. That the Phoenician alphabet, parent of all the European alphabets, was derived from an Atlantis alphabet, which was also conveyed from Atlantis to the Mayas of Central America.

11. That Atlantis was the original seat of the Aryan or Indo-European family of nations, as well as of the Semitic peoples, and possibly also of the Turanian races.

12. That Atlantis perished in a terrible convulsion of nature, in which the whole island sunk into the ocean, with nearly all its inhabitants.

13. That a few persons escaped in ships and on rafts, and carried to the nations east and west the tidings of the appalling catastrophe, which has survived to our own time in the Flood and Deluge legends of the different nations of the old and new worlds.

These propositions provide a glimpse of Donnelly's enthusiasm and single-mindedness, as well as of the scope of his study. He moves confidently through subjects involving biology, botany, ethnology, geology, geography, archaeology, art history, philology, religion, and mythology. And there are very few peoples and areas of the world that he does not bring under consideration at one time or another. But the propositions also hint at the general lack of critical judgment that pervades the book. On nearly every page there is an example of rash assumption, hasty conclusion, circular reasoning, or argument based purely in rhetoric. Many statements of fact are not fact at all, and in his enthusiastic drive to create his Atlantis he reveals a surprising naïveté. In his defense it should be pointed out that a great amount has been added to our knowledge of man's past since his time and he could not anticipate these new discoveries. But this does not excuse the rash, uncritical way in which Donnelly uses his material. De Camp has summed it up very well: "Since Donnelly's formidable learning is likely to stun the average reader into taking his statements at face value, a close look at his book is needed to show how careless, tendentious, and generally worthless it is."[31]

Unfortunately, we cannot look closely at Donnelly's book here, but perhaps an example or two chosen at random will help make the point. When comparing the civilizations of the Old and New Worlds, he observes: "If we find on both sides of the Atlantic precisely the same arts, sciences, religious beliefs, habits, customs, and traditions, it is absurd to say that the peoples of the two continents arrived separately, by precisely the same ends."[32] This kind of statement is, unfortunately, typical of the approach that many pro-Atlantists take toward their subject even today. Although in Donnelly's case the situation may be different, the rhetoric in a statement like this usually hides the fact that there is little of value in it. Actually, Donnelly's reasoning here, as so often, depends on a rather superficial consideration of the evidence. First of all, the arts, sciences, and the rest are not "precisely the same." To take just one example: the Europeans had wheeled vehicles and draught animals, while the New World did not. Moreover, things or habits appearing on both sides of the Atlantic can have separate origins. The similarity between the pyramids of Egypt and those of Central America, for example, which Donnelly and others cling to so tenaciously, is a superficial one. They may be vaguely similar in appearance, but in origin, construction, purpose, use, and chronology they are not connected. They were simply independent creations.

As far as the second half of his statement is concerned, it is generally believed nowadays that the peoples originally populating the New World came across the Bering Strait from Asia by way of a land bridge that was later submerged by the rising sea as the glaciers melted.

Another typically loose comparison is to be seen in his treatment of the Indian mounds of North America.[33] The mound builders were part of "the Atlantean American Empire," according to Donnelly, and their mounds provide significant evidence of a connection: "The chief characteristic of the Mound Builders was that from which they derived their name—the creation of great structures of earth or stone, not unlike the pyramids of Mexico and Egypt." Whether or not the mounds are their chief characteristic, the connection with Mexico and Egypt is hardly likely, since the mounds are quite unlike the pyramids of Mexico or Egypt and come from a different time. Donnelly's enthusiasm has carried him too far afield. This is also true of what he does with language. The gyrations he goes through to show "that the very word 'Olumpos' is a transformation from 'Atlantis'," for example, amount to nothing more than preposterous rationalizing.[34]

Donnelly's influence keeps appearing in the twentieth-century literature on Atlantis, sometimes with credit given and sometimes not. But at the same time those dealing with the subject have gone well beyond Donnelly—for better or for worse. At the one extreme are the occultists who have created whole new systems of philosophy based on Atlantis or incorporating Plato's island as an important element. These mystics—people like Helena Blavatsky and Edgar Cayce—are best ignored here, for they have little or nothing to contribute to solving the Atlantis question. They are simply users of Atlantis for their own purposes, and it is unfortunate that their ideas have not yet been completely laid to rest.

The majority of the literature on Atlantis falls into the category with Donnelly—books by well-meaning enthusiasts who usually have a theory to develop. Here mention must be made of Lewis Spence, whose book *The Problem of Atlantis,* which appeared in 1924, has been called "about the best pro-Atlantis work published to date."[35] And yet it too is full of misconceptions about chronology, geology, archaeology, and ethnography. Spence shows less naïveté than Donnelly and maintains a more controlled and rational approach, but his theories are no more tenable than Donnelly's. He posits a large continent in the north Atlantic until the end of the Miocene period when it began to disintegrate, leaving two islands, Atlantis and Antillia, some time later. The island was originally inhabited by a handsome and admirable Stone-Age people, the Crô-Magnons, who were in turn defeated by the Azilians who entered under the leadership of their culture hero, Poseidon. This brought the disintegration of the culture that Plato speaks of. Spence also finds connections between Atlantis and the Old and New Worlds, most of which are based on the same superficial comparisons that Donnelly found.

The creation of Antillia is an interesting new element. Since it was destroyed, according to Spence, after Atlantis, it served as a stepping-stone for the survivors to the New World. And so Antillia becomes a direct connection between Atlantis and America and at the same time provides a solution to the chronological problem arising from the fact that the advanced civilizations of Central and South America fall at a time much later than the destruction of Atlantis. The only problem is that there is no proof Antillia ever existed; it is a figment of Spence's imagination.

Spence's treatment of Crô-Magnon man is also faulty, for he transforms him from a Palaeolithic cave-dweller into a domesticated, horse-riding, village-dweller. "They had their cave-temples and their trades, their rulers and social grades."[36]

While Donnelly and Spence have their faults, they hardly measure up to Immanuel Velikovsky, who, shortly after the Second World War, came up with a bizarre theory of a comet that twice came close to the earth about 1500 B.C., causing catastrophes of all kinds.[37] Among these were the reversal of the earth's rotation and the sinking of Atlantis. His theories have not been taken very seriously and are better classed with science fiction.

There is not the time or space here to pursue the theories of other pro-Atlantis enthusiasts. It is worth noting, however, that while most people would still put it in the Atlantic, others have found Atlantis in places as far apart and widely different as the Arctic and Nigeria. Entries in this list include the Caucasus, Crimea, various places in North Africa, including the Sahara, Malta, a number of sites in Spain, Central France, Belgium, the Netherlands, the North Sea, the Bahamas, as well as different places in North and South America. Even a superficial glance through the various theories, however, suggests that, while some sophistication of knowledge and methods is apparent, the purposes and results remain what they had been earlier. No one identification has surfaced as solving the problem.

Besides the occultists and enthusiasts, there has also been a certain number of experts in the sciences who have approached the Atlantis problem at least tangentially. Here interesting new possibilities have been suggested to explain the disappearance of

Atlantis. The continental drift theory has led to the idea that America may be Atlantis. But this is not at all likely, since the rate of drift of the continents is very slow and such movement would have taken place at a time far too early for human memory to have recorded it.

Another idea that has been suggested is that an earthquake some distance away might have produced a tidal wave or a tsunami which inundated the island. But such a wave, while it could bring serious damage, especially along the coast, would not cause complete and permanent inundation of the island.[38]

Geologists and others have also proposed volcanic activity as the cause of the demise of Atlantis. The Azores, for example, are taken by some to be proof of this. But this idea too has been refuted.[39]

Proof of the earlier existence of an island in the Atlantic has been seen by some in the basaltic glass tachylite that has been dredged up from the ocean floor off the Azores. The belief that this substance could be formed only in the open air suggested to at least one expert that the land mass of which it was a part had originally been above water and had subsequently sunk. Although this idea keeps appearing in contemporary writing on Atlantis as something proving the existence and subsidence of the island, it is generally rejected by geologists, since it has been shown that tachylite can be formed under water as well as above. For that matter, as Dorothy Vitaliano points out below (p. 139), there is no geological evidence at all to show that any mass of land has sunk in the Atlantic as recently as 9600 B.C.[40]

Not very long ago it was suggested, almost in passing, by the geochemist Cesare Emiliani and others, that a sudden rise in sea level around 11,600 years ago caused by glacial meltwater could account not only for the inundation of Atlantis but also for the various flood legends that appear throughout the world.[41] There is considerable doubt whether there was any significant rise in sea level, but even if there was, the theory provides for a rise of only "decimeters per year," thus making it difficult to see how Atlantis would be suddenly inundated as Plato suggests. At the same time, the problem of cultural development remains. In 9600 B.C. man was in such a primitive state of development that it is impossible to imagine the deluge stories as beginning then and continuing to historical times.

Perhaps the most promising attempt to locate and identify Plato's Atlantis has come about in recent years as a by-product of archaeological research in Crete and the eastern Mediterranean. Dorothy Vitaliano has given a summary of these researches in her essay which follows (pp. 143–47), and John Luce has reevaluated Plato's story in the light of the archaeological research in his book *The End of Atlantis*. Four of the essays in the present collection involve this identification directly or indirectly.

It is clear that in 1450 B.C. or perhaps a little earlier there was a tremendous eruption on the island of Thera (Santorini), which lies a little more than sixty miles north of Crete. Ash which has been identified as coming from this eruption has been found in cores taken from a wide area of the eastern Mediterranean and on Crete as well. Although there is still much debate as to how destructive this eruption actually was as far as Crete was concerned, the theory that the destruction of Atlantis is reflected in this eruption has gained a number of adherents.

There is no need to repeat here what is well summarized below, but a few general observations are in order. If Atlantis is to be found or, perhaps to put it more fairly, if Plato's story is based on some kind of fact, then the Thera-Crete hypothesis does have promise. In the first place, archaeology has shown Crete to be a powerful island culture with one center, Knossos, predominating. It has also been pointed out that this island fits Plato's story in a number of other striking ways. These range all the way from similarities between the terrain and topography of Atlantis and Crete to striking congruence of details such as the importance of the bull in the religions of both. Plato's description of bull-hunting is remarkably similar to scenes on the well-known Vapheio cups which were made in Crete somewhere between 1500 and 1450 B.C.[42]

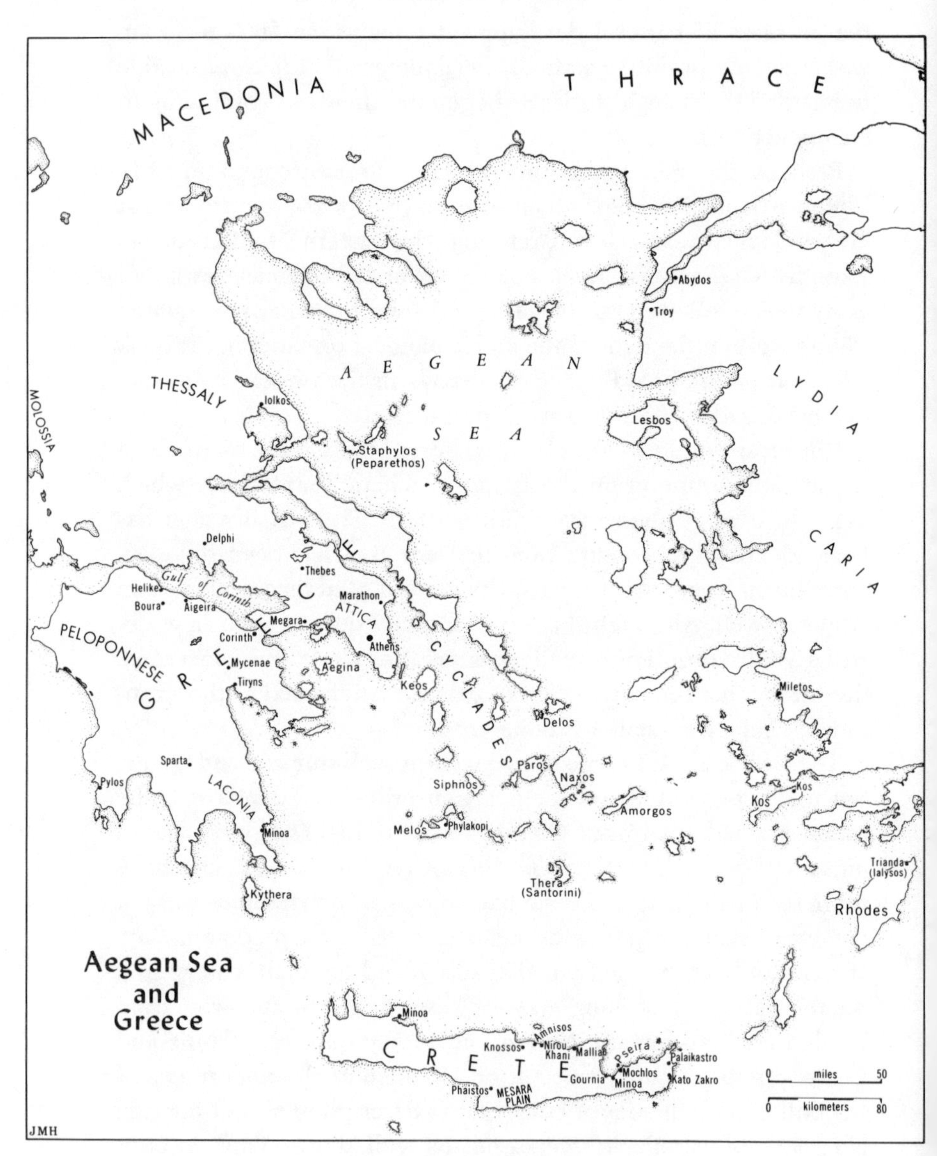

Crete and the Aegean.

The eruption that occurred on Thera is certainly the kind of natural disaster that Plato is talking about, but the date presents a problem; 1450 B.C. is hardly 9600 B.C. A few years ago A. G. Galanopoulos suggested that a mistake had been made in transmitting this and other numbers and that by the time they appeared in Plato's account they were ten times as large as they should have been. If this is correct, then the event occurred not 9,000 years before Solon, but 900 years earlier. If we take 550 or 600 B.C. as a rough but reasonable date for Solon's visit to Egypt, then Atlantis would have been destroyed about 1450 B.C. or just about the time of the great eruption on Thera. So convincing has the whole idea appeared to some that it has made its way into histories of Minoan art and culture without further comment.[43] But in the long history of the search for Atlantis theories popular at one moment sink into oblivion at the next, and one may well wonder whether Santorini-Crete-Atlantis will suffer the same fate.

When we deal with Atlantis we usually think of the theories and ideas of the pro-Atlantists. But as John Luce points out below (pp. 49–50), and as has already been indicated above, the non-believers have always been present. Their side, however, has not always been heard. Skeptics can be easily ignored, especially when a topic as mystical and emotionally charged as Atlantis is under consideration. People want to believe and will do so as long as there is the vaguest possibility that Atlantis ever existed. Each new theory prolongs hopes.

At the same time, the skeptics have not been as outspoken as the believers. Except for Martin in the last century and de Camp in more recent times, no one has attacked the Atlantis story in any detail. The classical scholars mentioned by John Luce just brush Atlantis aside. In fact, Jowett can barely bring himself to mention it. This attitude is extremely common among the experts.

On the scientific side a similar skepticism has surfaced from time to time. When Termier put forward his tachylite theory in 1912, for example, Charles Schuchert was quick to object. Using his own experience and that of his fellow scientists, Schuchert came to the following conclusions: "(1) that the Azores are volcanic islands and are not the remnants of a more or less large continental mass, for they are not composed of rocks seen on the continents; (2) that the tachylites dredged up from the Atlantic to the north of the Azores were in all probability formed where they are now, at the bottom of the ocean; and (3) that there are no known geologic data that prove or even help to prove the existence of Plato's Atlantis in historic times."[44]

Another geologist, William D. Matthew, in a report summarized in the *Proceedings of the National Academy of Sciences,* comes out against the land-bridge theory. He says that Plato's story is a fable and that "the scientific evidence does not lend any support to it nor vice-versa."[45]

The Americanist G. C. Vaillant expressed himself briefly but in no uncertain terms in a book review in 1949: "The culture of the American Indian is pitifully distorted when seen through the eyes of believers in a lost continent and lost civilization, be they Atlanteans who lost their continent in the Atlantic or Mu-ites whose magic civilization sank beneath the waves of the Pacific."[46] He repeated his skepticism a few years later in his book on the Aztecs of Mexico.[47]

L. Don Leet, the seismologist, took time out in his *Causes of Catastrophe* to devote a few pages to the story of Atlantis, which he calls an "all-time favorite among tall tales involving earthquakes, tidal waves and hurricanes." He points out that there is no evidence to suggest that any land mass has sunk in the Atlantic in the last 11,000 years.[48] Most recently there has been Herbert E. Wright's criticism of Emiliani's theories of sea-level rise, which have already been mentioned.[49] He elaborates his ideas in the final essay of this collection.

Perhaps it is already clear why those who are best qualified to speak about Atlantis are satisfied with offering incidental criticism or else ignore the problem entirely. The one common denominator among all the various theories that have been put forward is the singular lack of detachment shown by the theorists.

Instead of beginning with Plato, most begin with a hypothesis and develop their ideas with an enthusiasm that often verges on fanaticism. The logical extensions of this are occultism and science fiction, where Atlantis has been extremely popular.

This lack of detachment often combines with a less than adequate expertise in the disciplines drawn on and produces a generally poor use of evidence and even distortion of fact. If the ancient references to Atlantis are not simply ignored, for example, they are used indiscriminately for the immediate purpose without any consideration of the context of the statement and the motives and reliability of the ancient writer.

Perhaps the most flagrant abuse of the ancient sources is seen in the treatment of Plato himself, in spite of the fact that he is our primary source and perhaps our only independent authority for the Atlantis story. Although the philosopher gives a clear date and position for Atlantis, the island—if indeed it is left as an island—is shifted about in time and space according to the whims of the particular person writing about it. For some it is not enough to accept what Plato says by way of description, but they have to make this island the source of all civilization. At the same time, Athens is ignored, even though Plato's whole purpose in telling this story is to illustrate the efficacy of the social, political, and military systems that ostensibly existed in the city at this early date. Even those promoting perhaps the most carefully developed theory, that of Santorini-Minoan Crete mentioned earlier, are forced to deviate from Plato's account in a number of important respects. Atlantis has been moved from the Atlantic Ocean to the Eastern Mediterranean; the date has been arbitrarily changed from 9,000 years before Solon to 900 years before his time; an island that did not sink has been substituted for one that did.

And the methods of the Atlantis enthusiasts are in many cases not very reasonable. Some of the shortcomings of Spence's work have already been indicated. To a large extent these stem from the way in which he goes about his investigation. Early in his history of Atlantis Spence observes: "It must be manifest how great a part inspiration has played in the disentangling of archaeological problems during the last century." After mentioning the decipherment of Egyptian hieroglyphics and the Near Eastern cuneiform script and referring to Schliemann's discovery of Troy, he goes on: "Inspirational methods, indeed, will be found to be those of the Archaeology of the Future. The Tape-Measure School, dull and full of the credulity of incredulity, is doomed."[50] There is no point in dwelling on what "The Tape-Measure School" has contributed to our knowledge of the past. What is more important is the anti-intellectual feeling that is hinted at here. By now this has blossomed in some pro-Atlantis circles to the point where the experts are often brushed aside with a show of rhetoric and ideas are repeated that have been shown to have no basis in fact. The result is often an appealing but generally preposterous picture, such as large and beautiful cities existing 11,500 years ago when men were actually living in caves and still hunting or gathering their food. It is one of the ironies of the search for Atlantis that Plato, who lies at the center of our intellectual tradition, now finds himself in many cases the victim of an anti-intellectual approach.

Another rather common mistake that the Atlantists make is to explain one unknown by using or creating another. Here, of course, the early geographers come to mind. But a more recent example of this is the connection often made between Atlantis and the Maya. There are many questions about Mayan origins and development that remain unanswered. The less that is known about both sides, the easier it is to hypothesize, and once the idea has appeared in print, it is a logical next step to treat it as fact.

By now it is perhaps unnecessary to point out that the driving desire to explain Atlantis at all costs has also been responsible for a great deal of out-and-out rationalizing and wild theorizing without any evidence at all. As we have seen, Spence created a whole new island, Antillia, to get his Atlanteans to the New World at the proper time after the destruction of their island. Folk memory, movements of peoples in Central Asia, comets, Atlantis the source of all civilization, land bridges, and whole continents in the north

Atlantic are just a few of the many devices that have been invented to explain different aspects of various theories.

The result of all this has been a rather strange intriguing footnote in the history of human thought. Man loves the mysterious and the insoluble, and so he has been attracted to Atlantis. Much has been written and new books appear every day. This proliferation of writing on the subject shows that no one has yet offered a satisfactory solution to the problem—if, that is, there is a problem at all.

THE LITERARY PERSPECTIVE

The Sources and Literary Form of Plato's Atlantis Narrative

JOHN V. LUCE

The general public continues to believe in Atlantis, but the prevailing attitude among classical philologists has long been one of skepticism. Benjamin Jowett was representative of much nineteenth-century scholarship when he wrote in his introduction to the *Critias*: "Hence we may safely conclude that the entire narrative is due to the imagination of Plato."[1] J. A. Stewart, in his pioneering study of the myths, concurred with this verdict: "Atlantis, I take it, is a creature of Plato's own imagination."[2] In the twenties and thirties of this century, F. M. Cornford and A. E. Taylor both produced commentaries on the *Timaeus*, and both held that the Atlantis legend was a mere fiction.[3]

In France, at that time, leading scholars were equally skeptical. A. Rivaud, the editor of the *Timaeus* and *Critias* in the Budé series, thought that the myth of Atlantis, and consequently the whole of the *Critias*, were *simples fables*.[4] Rivaud distinguished clearly between the geological and historical issues raised by Plato's narrative. Undoubtedly there have been geological cataclysms in the past, but they do not enter into the domain of history unless they can be shown to have affected the progress of civilization. The possible submergence of a land mass in the Atlantic Ocean is a geological issue and should be left to scientists to settle. But Plato's picture of the high civilization of the people of Atlantis and their aggression against the peoples of the eastern Mediterranean raises questions of quite a different order. No one, he said, had mentioned these matters before Plato, so far as we know. He therefore concluded: "All probabilities are in favor of Plato's having invented the whole history of Atlantis."[5] P. Frutiger, in his brilliant survey of the Platonic myths, fastened on "the two essential characteristics" in the Atlantis narrative, namely, the war of the Atlanteans against Greece, and the sudden disappearance of their island under the sea. There could be no question here, he thought, of any tradition related to actual events. A tradition "purely legendary" was admissible in principle, but very improbable in fact. Besides these distinctive features, Plato, he pointed out, also introduced themes utilized in other myths, such as the Age of Gold, the autochthonous origin of the Athenians, and the periodic destructions of mankind. Since these themes are obviously mythical, they create a presumption in favor of the fabulous character of the whole recital.[6]

The skeptical case has been strongly presented, but there has always been a minority of scholars prepared to entertain the possibility that Plato in his Atlantis narrative utilized materials not entirely devoid of historical content. It seems clear, for example, that Plato took seriously the notion of periodic setbacks in civilization due to major natural disasters. This view appears in a non-mythical context in the *Laws* (677a). It could be argued that for Plato world floods or world conflagrations were facts of history, and that he thought their reality was confirmed by "myths" like those of Deucalion or Phaethon, which he cites in the *Timaeus* (22a-c). In other words, he interpreted these myths as picturesque representations of events that actually occurred.[7]

Now the theme of destruction by earthquake and sea-flood is an integral part of the story of Atlantis. This being so, it may well be an oversimplification to attribute such a detail merely to Plato's imagination. One should not rule out the possibility that he had a source for it. It might be argued that Plato was wrong to suppose that civilization was ever destroyed by a flood, but then the argument is about the relation between myth and history. In any *a priori* rejection of the Atlantis narrative as a complete fiction, one would have to maintain that myths *never* reflect historical fact.

In this essay I do not interpret the quest for Atlantis as the quest for the location of a lost island. The search for Atlantis in this sense has generated an immense literature, much of it very unscholarly. For me the quest for Atlantis is a problem in source criticism. Did Plato use any sources for the composition of his tale of Atlantis? If so, what were they and did they have any historical content irrespective of what Plato may have made of them?

If the problem is posed in this way, it will be seen that one cannot brusquely terminate the endeavors of source criticism by brandishing terms like "fantasy" or "imagination." One should take a hard look at the possibility that Plato really did utilize some Egyptian source material with a historical content. It is this possibility which down the centuries has put a brake on total skepticism and has restrained a small but respectable minority of scholars from rejecting the Atlantis legend as a "mere fable."

Ancient editorial comment on these lines is reviewed below. Theophrastus and Posidonius must also be added to the list of ancient scholars who thought that the legend was at least partly grounded in fact.[8] Among modern editors, Stallbaum was prepared to credit Plato's use of Egyptian sources, and Martin, in the "Dissertation sur l'Atlantide" included in his celebrated work on the *Timaeus*, thought that Plato might have been inspired by "an Egyptian tradition."[9] The sober Grote recognized that "the line between truth and fiction was obscurely drawn in his [Plato's] mind," and thought it "not improbable that Solon did leave an unfinished Egyptian poem," while H. Berger took "Egyptian accounts" to be one important element in the materials which Plato assembled for the construction of his narrative.[10] L. Robin claimed that Atlantis was not entirely mythical, and J. B. Skemp, while allowing that the story might be "largely Plato's own imaginative fiction," found it "hard to believe that there was no basis for it in legend."[11]

This long-standing scholarly dissension about the "authenticity" of the legend may indicate that the questions have not always been posed in the most appropriate way. Atlantis: fact or fiction? Like a witness in court we are expected to be able to answer "Yes, it is fact," or "No, it is fantasy." But I would urge that it is wrong to look for such an all-or-nothing verdict when considering a Platonic myth. In the myths of Plato we are faced with a literary form which resists any curt and sweeping imposition of the categories of truth or falsity. In the elaboration of their details the myths obviously exhibit a fictional element, but in their overall construction they are vehicles for conveying the truth as Plato sees it. In assessing them we should not be too quick to impose our work-a-day oppositions between "fact" and "fiction." Ultimately, I believe, the full comprehension of a Platonic myth requires us to transcend the truth/falsity antithesis, at least as commonly conceived.

Such an approach is no novelty in Platonic exegesis. It can be traced back as far as Iamblichus (about A.D. 300) on the evidence of Proclus' commentary on the *Timaeus*.[12] Proclus rejects the naïve view that the Atlantis legend is "plain history," a view apparently held by Crantor, the first editor of the *Timaeus*. But he equally rejects the other extreme, that it is a "mere fiction." Proclus favors the view of Iamblichus and his own teacher Syrianus that the conflict between Athens and Atlantis is not to be dismissed as unhistorical. We should allow, he thinks, that some such struggle did take place. But the significance of the story does not derive solely from the historicity of the remote conflict that it reports. The materials of the legend should be given an enlarged reference. They should be seen as embodying and symbolizing a cosmic contest inherent in the nature of the universe.[13] Iamblichus and his Neoplatonist followers clearly took a grandiose view of the legend, but anything less may fail to do it justice in the context of Plato's vision of the past.

The Atlantis legend forms an integral part of a grand compositional design. The *Timaeus,* with its introductory outline of the legend, is generally thought to have constituted the first member of a planned trilogy of dialogues. *Three* distinguished men, who are to deliver discourses as a repayment to Socrates for his *Republic,* are formally introduced at the outset (*Timaeus* 20a). Timaeus expounds the genesis of the cosmos and the origin of mankind. The stage is thus set for Critias to introduce the drama of ancient history with his narrative of the great war between Athens and Atlantis. But Plato left the *Critias* unfinished, and there is no trace of a *Hermocrates.* We can only speculate about what it might have contained. A possible theme for it would have been the strategy and prospects of the Hellenic world in the continuing struggle against the "barbarians."

With good reason Cornford calls this the "most ambitious design" that Plato ever conceived.[14] Its purpose was to present a panorama of the crucial stages in the history of the world from the creation down to Plato's own time. The war between the ancient Athenians and the Atlanteans is given an important place in this historical pageant. I find it very hard to believe that it was regarded as a complete fiction by Plato himself.[15] Given his overall design, would Plato have included a story which he himself had invented from beginning to end, and which he knew to be fictitious through and through? "Listen to my story," says Critias (*Timaeus* 20d), "it is strange but absolutely true." Would Plato have introduced the tale in such a way if he had known it to be entirely without historical foundation? I do not think he would.

There is, of course, a touch of irony in the phrase "strange but absolutely true." Critias is a devout traditionalist—I take him to be the Critias who was Plato's great-grandfather, not Critias the "tyrant" (see Appendix, p. 76). Plato is deftly characterizing him by making him insist on the complete authenticity of a legendary tale with a mainly oral foundation. We probably come closer to Plato's own attitude to the legend in the comment put into the mouth of Socrates (*Timaeus* 26e): "The theme is very appropriate to the festival of the goddess, and it's a considerable advantage that it happens to be a true account and not a fictitious tale." The goddess is Athena, and the festival is probably one of the Panathenaic festivals. It was therefore appropriate to recall a notable incident in the past history of Athens. The tendency of panegyrists on such occasions would be to exaggerate, and Socrates shows himself aware of this in his detached and again slightly ironic comment. I suggest that "Socrates" is here the mouthpiece for Plato's own reflections on his source materials and the use he is making of them. In other words, I am suggesting that Plato accepts a core of truth in the Atlantis legend, while claiming the license of a eulogist to work it up in a context where national pride must be flattered.

One of the main functions of the narrative is to show a city like the Ideal State of the *Republic* involved in political and military action. As Critias puts it: "I shall then, in accordance with Solon's enactment as well as with his story, bring them [that is, the citizens of the Ideal State] before our tribunal and make them our fellow-citizens, on the plea that they are those old Athenians of whose disappearance we are informed by the report of the sacred writings."[16] Socrates had outlined an ideal regime in the *Republic*, and early in the *Timaeus* (19b-c) he is made to express a desire to see the figures he has delineated brought to life and movement as they take part in the struggle for survival. This wish of Socrates foreshadows one of the important motifs of the *Timaeus* (37c), that the world is "a living and moving image of the immortal gods." In the visible cosmos ideal patterns are bodied forth in time and motion. After describing the cosmogonic process in these terms, Plato moves on in the *Critias* to interpret the historical process in a similar way. There are ideal patterns for constitutions, military organization, education, and so on. The more adequately such patterns are realized in actual states, the more their affairs will prosper, and the more admiration they will win from those who contemplate their achievements. This is the conceptual frame that underlies the *Timaeus* and *Critias* alike, and makes them a "reasonable story" and a "true account" respectively.[17]

The *Timaeus* appealed to the Hellenizing Jews at Alexandria because they detected a parallel between the *Demiourgos* (Maker of the World) and the Creator God of Genesis. In a famous phrase Eusebius later summed up these attitudes when he called Plato "Moses writing in Attic Greek."[18] In a similar vein of comparison I would suggest that there is a structural parallel between the *Timaeus-Critias* and Genesis. In Genesis, after the account of the creation, the next theme is the state of the world before the Flood. Plato follows a similar scheme. After describing the fashioning of the cosmos in the *Timaeus,* he moves on in the *Critias* to expatiate on what happened in antediluvian times. The author of Genesis is no romancer. He is part poet, part chronicler. It is my contention that Plato exhibits these two functions also, and operates in both these modes in his presentation of the material of the *Timaeus-Critias.*

Plato did not succeed in realizing his planned trilogy. A plausible explanation of his failure is that he decided to make a fresh start with the presentation of the material. The result is that detailed appraisal of human history, culture, and legislation which we know as the *Laws.* Book 3 of the *Laws* contains an account of the remote past of mankind that shares a number of significant features with *Timaeus-Critias.* There is a common emphasis on the immense span of time involved in human tradition, on the loss of detailed records from the earlier stages of man's development, and on the periodic setbacks he experiences from fire and flood.[19]

At the beginning of *Laws* Book 3 (677a-b) the Athenian Stranger (generally agreed to be a mouthpiece for Plato himself) asks his companions whether they do not agree that the "old stories contain some truth." When questioned as to what stories he has in mind, he replies: "The accounts of many disasters through floods, plagues, and so on, as a result of which only small remnants of mankind survived." Cleinias agrees that these legends are very plausible. The Stranger then proceeds to envisage the few "shepherds in the mountains" who survived the Great Flood. This passage is very reminiscent of the discourse of the Egyptian priest in the *Timaeus* (22b-d). Like the Stranger, the priest begins from the premise that there have been many major disasters through fire and flood, and he refers to the "herdsmen and shepherds in the mountains" who escape the periodic inundations. As an instance of destruction by fire, he refers to the Greek legend of Phaethon and the chariot of Helios. The story, he says, has "the form of a myth," but embodies the truth that over long periods of time the heavenly bodies may deviate from their normal courses and cause destruction by overheating on the earth's surface.

In view of these similarities it is not, I think, sound to classify the Atlantis legend as "mythical" (if that implies "fictional") while treating *Laws* Book 3 as "historical." Both presentations embody a coherent theory of historical process. The categories of the theory provide a framework within which Plato attempts to bring some order into the tangled detritus of Greek mythology.

Further evidence of this characteristic approach of Plato in his late period is provided by the opening remarks of the *Politicus* myth (268e-269b). There Plato finds evidence for an astronomical "happening" (*pathos*), the prehistoric reversal of the sun's orbit, in the legend of Thyestes. We may also point to a striking remark put into the mouth of Critias (*Critias* 110a): "Storytelling (*muthologia*) and the investigation of the remote past appeared in the cities with the growth of leisure." Storytelling is here put on a par with historical inquiry. The *muthos*, or story, for Plato is not a fiction; it embodies the traditions of mankind's past.

R. Weil is one of the few scholars in this century to make a case for something like "systematic historiography" in the later dialogues.[20] Plato the historian! He has rarely been called that. Most scholars tend to regard his world view as unhistorical, if not antihistorical. Two of Weil's reviewers put succinctly the main reasons for this assessment. According to G. B. Kerferd, Plato is usually regarded as a bad historian because (1) "the truth he is seeking is philosophic truth and not the truth of historical occurrence in time"; and because (2) he seems "incurably frivolous in his treatment of historical events, ever ready to mix fiction with truth and to manipulate the record to suit his purpose." C. H. Kahn adds a third reason: (3) "In the last analysis, Plato is not interested in history at all but in its lessons."[21]

All these reasons can, and should, be questioned. Reason (1) is broadly true of the *Republic.* Here, more than in any other dialogue, Plato draws a firm line between appearance and reality, between imagination and thought. There is more depreciation of "myth," while the saving power of "reason" is correspondingly exalted. This is a product of the strong vein of dogmatic idealism in Plato's thought at the time. Since the *Republic* is the best known of Plato's writings, the low estimate of legends there given, especially when narrated by poets, has tended to impress itself on critics as his considered view. However, in the post-*Republic* dialogues there is a marked change of emphasis in Plato's attitude to the phenomenal world. He now recognizes that reality is not frozen in immobility like a statue, however hallowed and revered, but that "change" and "life" must be included in it (*Sophist* 248e–249a). Particular objects are no longer depreciated as mere sources of illusion, but are to be inspected and classified as a basis for the apprehension of Forms. In the *Laws* there is what G. R. Morrow well calls a "descent into the arena of practical difficulties."[22] The "city in heaven" of the *Republic* is replaced by a colony in the Messara plain eighty stades from the sea.

This change of attitude encompassed the particular events of past history. There is a revealing passage in the *Laws* (682a) where Plato comments on the significance of the founding of Dardania as described by Homer. The poets, he now allows, with "the aid of the Graces and Muses" are able to comprehend "many events that really happened." The legends poets record can further the philosophical inquirer in his efforts to detect and formulate the laws and main stages of political and social development.

What is said about poetry in general, and about Homer in particular, in this passage of the *Laws* stands in marked contrast to the depreciation of poetic *mimesis* (imitation) in *Republic* Book 10.[23]

Reason (2) for denying Plato the title of historian seems also to rest on too narrow a selection of texts. It seems, in fact, to be largely based on the *Menexenus,* where the notes of parody and satire are strongly sounded. Plato is there poking fun at the conventional eulogies of Athenian fame which tended to distort and misuse history. He is showing that he can play at that game too. But just as one would not take the *Euthydemus* very seriously in an overall assessment of Plato as a philosopher, so, I suggest, one should place little store by the *Menexenus* as indicative of Plato's lack of historical insight. A very different impression is given by Plato's version of Peloponnesian history, again from *Laws* Book 3. After discussing this in detail, Morrow concludes: "Our survey has failed to show any important instances in which Plato has distorted facts in the interests of theory."[24] Plato, he continues, shows a striking "loyalty to history" in his account of the evolution of the Spartan constitution.

Reason (3), like the first, is too sharply antithetical. Plato was certainly interested in the lessons of history, but it does not follow that he had no interest in the past for its own sake. Even in the *Republic* (486a) he says that the philosopher should aim at a synoptic vision of all *time* and all reality. Here we may detect the germ of the historical approach which Weil and Morrow find so amply deployed in the later dialogues, especially the *Laws.* Kahn rather gives his case away when he allows that Plato offers us a "schematic account of the past."[25] What more, one might retort, does Thucydides give us in his "Archaeology"?

Let us return to the *Critias* narrative of Atlantis and Athens and consider into what genre it falls. Such an approach may help to reinforce the contention that it is designed as history rather than as fable. It is, I think, significant that Plato *never* calls it a *muthos,* but always a *logos.*[26] This point tends to be overlooked by those who classify it with the eschatological "myths" of the middle period dialogues, or the cosmographical "myth" of the *Politicus*. My suggestion, which I have not seen previously made, is that it should be classified as a "panegyric discourse" (*logos panegurikos*) on a par with the *Panathenaicus* of Isocrates or the *Funeral Oration* of Lysias.

There are a number of details in the text which support this suggestion. Critias the speaker is a senior Athenian statesman (see Appendix, p. 76). The occasion is a festival of Athena, and the "great and marvelous exploits" of the city are to be recalled as a fitting "encomium" for the occasion.[27] (Detailed allusions to the ancient exploits of Athens were a commonplace of the panegyric genre.[28]) Critias begins with an epideictic commonplace. He asks, at somewhat inordinate length, for the indulgence of his audience since he is about to undertake a task of considerable difficulty.[29] The audience is twice called a "theatre" (*Critias* 108b, 108d), encouraging us to imagine the speech as delivered to a large group in a public place of assembly. Finally, the arrangement of the contents follows the prescription given in the *Menexenus*: first, the noble lineage of the ancient worthies is given; then, their nurture and education is described; thirdly, the great deeds they accomplished are recounted.[30]

Assuming, then, that there is a case for regarding the *Critias* as cast in the standard *form* of a panegyric oration, what inference can we make about its *contents*? It seems to me that Plato composing in this vein would have made some effort to base his eulogy on fact rather than fantasy. A eulogist of Athens had license to enhance the kudos of the citizens past and present, but he would be expected to take his starting point in something the city had done, or was generally believed to have done. It would be no compliment to praise Athens for a completely fictitious exploit. Now, in the matter of the ancient victory over Atlantis, it is unlikely that there was any popular tradition about such an exploit current in the Athens of Plato's day.[31] As Critias explains at the outset (*Timaeus* 21d): "Because of the lapse of time . . . the story has not survived *here* [that is, in Athens]." The Atlantis narrative is designed to take its audience back beyond the reach of current

Greek legend. Only in Egypt, where a written tradition gave access to a past very remote by Greek standards, could such a story have been preserved. It then becomes a crucial question whether we can place any reliance on the Egyptian pedigree of the legend. Could Solon, or Plato, have picked up any hint or outline of such a story from Egyptian sources?

There are biographical traditions, based on good evidence, that both men did visit Egypt. In the case of Solon, the best testimony is a fragment of his own poetry in which he mentions the Canopic mouth of the Nile.[32] The line as preserved does not actually say that he saw what he describes, but it is quoted by Plutarch to confirm the tradition of the Egyptian journey (*Life of Solon* 26.1). Presumably the complete poem made it clear that Solon did visit the Nile delta. The tradition runs back to Plato, himself a descendant of Solon (see Appendix, p. 76), who states unequivocally that his great ancestor did visit Saïs and was well received by the priests of the goddess Neïth (*Timaeus* 21e–22a). At the time of the visit (about 593/2 B.C.) it was the policy of the Saïte dynasty to encourage the Greek presence in Egypt through concessions to the "treaty-port" of Naucratis. Solon could easily have taken ship to Naucratis, which lay on the Canopic branch of the Nile, and from there to Saïs was a distance of only about sixteen kilometers. Psammetichos I had established a school for interpreters to facilitate intercourse between the two races, so there would have been no major obstacle to communication. Given Solon's wide cultural interests and lively Athenian curiosity, he might be expected to have sought contact with the temple priests, who were the archivists and antiquarians of ancient Egypt.

The case for Plato's visit to Egypt rests primarily on what he says in the *Laws* about Egyptian art and customs (656d–657a, 747c, 799a–b, 819a–d, 953e). I follow Wilamowitz, Bidez, and others in regarding these passages as based on firsthand knowledge of the country.[33] The effect of the passages is cumulative, but perhaps the single most telling reference is the account of the conservatism of Egyptian art forms (656d–657a). The Athenian

Stranger tells Cleinias that Egyptian art is "a marvel even to hear about," and continues: "If you look, you will find there paintings and sculptures ten thousand years old—not 'roughly' but 'really' ten thousand years old—which are in no way more beautiful or uglier than the products of contemporary artists, but wrought with the same expertise." This passage smacks of the traveled eyewitness. Given that Plato did reside for some time in Egypt, we may accept the force of Wilamowitz's further contention that the country made a great impression on Plato and that he was particularly struck by the respect accorded to the priestly caste.[34] In such an ordering of society he would have seen a practical instance of his ideal of the "rule of intelligence" in the person of the "philosopher-priest." He will also have noted, as Herodotus did (2.164–166), the separate life and privileges of the military caste. Such observations may well have provided some of the inspiration for the class structure worked out in the *Republic*, which, like the Egyptian system, was designed to have a strong stabilizing effect on all social and political institutions.[35]

In his Egyptian journey, financed, perhaps, as Plutarch says (*Life of Solon* 2.8), by a cargo of olive oil from his Attic estate, Plato was following in the footsteps of illustrious predecessors. In addition to Solon, Hecataeus and Herodotus had also visited Egypt and had been much impressed by what they saw and heard there. Herodotus became convinced, like Plato, that Egyptian traditions in art and history went back for ten thousand years and more, and that "nothing had changed" in this long period.[36] The temple priests persuaded Herodotus to accept a figure of 11,340 years as the span of time covered by the rule of the Pharaohs and claimed to have documentary evidence for the whole period (Herodotus 2.142, 2.145). This figure is of the same order as the 9,000 years that Plato gives, again on priestly authority, for the lapse of time since Atlantis flourished and was overwhelmed.[37]

There is no call to juggle with the figures by knocking off a zero and referring the resulting 900 years to the time gap between the Bronze Age Thera eruption (about 1500 B.C.) and Solon's visit to

Egypt (about 600 B.C.).[38] In a previous treatment of the "date" of Atlantis I discussed the speculation that "Solon, or the priests, could have mistakenly multiplied some actual dates and linear measurements by ten."[39] My present view is that Plato is responsible for the dating in that he followed and accepted Egyptian estimates which projected the antiquity of the Pharaonic system back over ten millennia; 9,000 years, I now think, is his round figure way of indicating an "early" date by Egyptian standards.

Egyptian monuments could also have furnished historical hints to Plato. His stay in Egypt is likely to have been of some months' duration at least and to have included visits to Memphis and Heliopolis as well as to Saïs. Ramesside temples in lower Egypt have not survived, but there are sure indications that they existed.[40] Presumably the great temple which Ramesses II dedicated to Ptah at Memphis will have been adorned with reliefs depicting the triumphs of the Pharaoh in battle against foreign enemies. Battle scenes of this type are still vividly impressive to the modern tourist at Karnak or Medinet Habu. To a keen visualizer like Plato they would have conveyed a graphic picture of ancient Egypt under attack by invaders from distant lands. In the well-known reliefs of the Sea Peoples who menaced Egypt by land and sea with a massive force about 1191 B.C., the invaders do not at all resemble uncouth barbarians.[41] They are shown as well-armed fighters in well-equipped ships. Similar reliefs could well have furnished Plato with the nucleus of his Atlantis theme, the idea of a massive invasion of the eastern Mediterranean by an island empire of the West. The Atlantean armada was launched, it should not be forgotten, against Egypt as well as Hellas. (*Timaeus* 25b).

If Plato inquired in more detail about the exploits of Pharaohs like Sethos I, Ramesses II, or Ramesses III, he would almost certainly have received a very misleading account of their dating. One can infer as much from the Egyptian "history" of Herodotus in which the pyramid builders, though correctly named, are placed toward the end of the Pharaonic succession (2.124–134), and the great conqueror Sesostris is dated to a much earlier epoch (2.102–

110). "Sesostris" is a composite figure, but he must incorporate some aspects of the warrior Pharaohs of the New Kingdom, whose careers came a thousand years later than Cheops. Herodotus has in effect turned the course of Egyptian history back to front, presumably misled by informants like the scribe at the temple of Neïth in Saïs, or the priests of Heliopolis, whom he respected as "most versed in the traditions" of their country (2.28, 2.3).

In his discussion of Plato's sources, Proclus writes (*In Timaeum* 24B): "The temple-spokesmen of the Egyptians bear witness to these matters [that is, the story of the Athenians and Atlanteans], as he says, saying that they are recorded in writing on inscribed monuments (*stelae*) that are still preserved." Unfortunately the identity of "he" in the clause "as he says," is not absolutely certain. It is usual to take the subject to be Crantor, the first editor of the *Timaeus* in the generation after Plato's death. Crantor has been named by Proclus a few lines higher up. This seems to me to be the most natural rendering of the Greek, with the "as he says" of line 8 (Diehl) resuming the "as he says" of line 2 (Diehl). If this is correct, Proclus has preserved an important early testimony, independent of Plato's dialogues, for Egyptian influence on the Atlantis legend. It is possible to take the subject of "as he says" to be Plato, as Festugière does in his translation.[42] In that case, the whole sentence will merely be an inference by Proclus based on the Egyptian setting of the narrative. However, Festugière's rendering seems to be less likely, and I am prepared to accept that the information about the inscribed monuments goes back to Crantor.

At all events, it is plausible to picture Plato as gathering some historical information, however garbled, just as Herodotus did. By inspection of monuments and by conversation with temple-spokesmen, Plato can hardly have failed to learn something about Egypt in the Bronze Age. His firm grasp of the significance of the god Theuth (=Thoth), who is *not* mentioned by Herodotus, is clear from the Egyptian tale inserted in the *Phaedrus* (274c–275b). In the same tale he connects the god Ammon with Thebes and pictures the king of Thebes as ruler of all Egypt. One cannot then dismiss the *Phaedrus* tale as purely fictitious. On the contrary, it confirms that Plato was well informed about the religion and history of Egypt. But he would have had no way of synchronizing Egyptian historical data with the legendary past of his own country. Accepting, as he did, the standard Greek view of the great antiquity of Egypt, he would not have been disposed to downdate events like the Sea Peoples' raids to the epoch of the Trojan War. It must have seemed to him that the Hellenes were indeed "children," as the old priest said to Solon—young in years and experience in comparison with the ancient civilization of the Nile valley.

In the course of some reflections on Solon's poetic ability, Plato canvasses the reasons for his failure to "complete" or "work up" the story he acquired in Egypt. It is suggested that the turbulent condition of Athenian politics gave him no leisure for the task.[43] There is no indication, in the *Timaeus* at least, that Solon did other than transmit the tale *orally*. Critias repeatedly insists that he "heard" the tale from his grandfather, who in turn had it from the lips of Solon (*Timaeus* 20e, 25d–e). Only in the *Critias* do we hear of a Solonian manuscript (113a–b). The two dialogues are not necessarily inconsistent on this point. The manuscript, we are told, contained a list of names which Solon had established by inquiry as the Greek equivalents of those used in Egyptian documents. We are not told that it contained any more than a mere list of names, designed as an *aide memoire* by Solon for his projected epic poem on the Atlantis legend. However, despite Critias' assertion that the manuscript had been in his grandfather's possession and was still among his own papers, we should, I think, remain skeptical about it. It looks as though Plato introduced it in the *Critias* as an afterthought to explain the Greekness of the proper names in his pedigree of the royal house of Atlantis.

If there was no Solonian manuscript of Atlantis, was there even a Solonian oral report about the island? In my previous treatment of these questions, I was inclined, following the example of K. T. Frost, to attach considerable weight to the Solonian pedigree of the legend. I was inclined to accept what I call Frost's "crucial contention" that "Solon really did hear a tale in Saïs which filled him with wonder and which was really the true but misunderstood record of the Minoans." "Solon," I wrote, "plays a key role in the transmission of the legend as recorded by Plato" (*The End of Atlantis*, pp. 56, 37).

I still think that the figure of Solon is significant in the *presentation* of the legend. His reputation would impart a cachet of respectability to the tale, thus furthering Plato's intention to present it as history rather than fiction. The fact that he had visited Egypt would also serve to underline the Egyptian inspiration of the account. Solon in Egypt would, of course, have reacted much as Herodotus or Plato. He would have realized that Egyptian records preserved a documentary "window on the past" with a longer perspective than was available from any Greek source. It is not out of the question to suppose that Solon fashioned stories out of what he learned in Egypt, that a version of these became traditional in the family of Critias, and that Plato decided to give the tradition a wider currency.

The line of transmission by hearsay from Solon to Plato is long and thin, but not chronologically impossible (see Appendix, p. 76). Whether any information passed along it is, I now feel, very much open to doubt. My present view is that Solon and Critias figure in the presentation of the Atlantis legend much as Parmenides and Socrates figure in the *Parmenides*. In the latter case, the philosophical problems are Plato's, but he has chosen to present them in the dramatic form of a conversation between the historical Parmenides and a youthful Socrates. It is extremely unlikely that the two men ever met, and impossible that they could have held a discussion in the terms that Plato represents them as using. Why then does Plato set the scene in the way he does? The answer seems to be that Plato feels an intellectual kinship with both thinkers: with Parmenides as an idealist and a monist; with Socrates as a perpetual seeker for the universal element in thought and conduct. In view of this affiliation he allows himself the dramatic license of putting his own speculations into their mouths. Similarly, in the Atlantis narrative, the construction, the emphasis, and the concept of the past implied are Plato's. But he feels at liberty to father the discourse on Critias and Solon because they are his ancestors, because they are both distinguished Athenians, and because Solon was the first notable Greek statesman and writer to visit Egypt.

My present view, then, is that one should mentally substitute Plato for Solon as the authority for the Egyptian provenance of the legend, just as one credits Plato, not Parmenides, with the argumentation of the *Parmenides,* and Plato, not Socrates, with the positive teaching of the *Republic.* It was Plato, following in the footsteps of his distinguished ancestor, who came to Saïs and "was much honored by the Saïtes and questioned the priestly authorities there about past events" (*Timaeus* 21e–22a). It was Plato who tried out on them his theories about Phoroneus and Deucalion, and who "attempted to put these Greek myths in a chronological framework" (*Timaeus* 22a–b). It was Plato who worked up the materials of the Atlantis legend on the basis of his personal knowledge of Egyptian antiquities and contacts with its temple-spokesmen.

In his chronological setting of the events he was influenced, as I have argued above, by the image of the great antiquity of Egyptian civilization that had been fostered by Herodotus. Vidal-Naquet detects a direct reminiscence of Herodotus in the phrase "great and marvelous deeds of the city," which occurs in the opening sentences of the *Timaeus* summary.[44] Herodotus, too, at the start of his *History* states his intention to record "the great and marvelous deeds accomplished by Greeks and foreign peoples," and to rescue them from oblivion. Plato claims the same motivation in his account of the great war between prehistoric Athens and Atlantis. Following Herodotus also, he assumes the identity of Athena with the goddess Neïth, an identification which enables him to credit Athens with a past even longer than that of Saïs.[45]

To interpret the Egyptian background of the narrative in this way is to keep well within the bounds of reasonable conjecture.

To go further (as I did in *The End of Atlantis*), and to hypothesize that Plato acquired some garbled information about *Minoan Crete* from Egyptian sources, is to venture on less firm ground. A Minoan basis for the Atlantis legend was first proposed by K. T. Frost in 1909, and the hypothesis was further elaborated by S. Marinatos.[46] On balance I still think it more probable than not that Egyptian traditions about Bronze Age Crete formed a significant part of the material acquired by Plato in Egypt. On the available evidence this hypothesis can never reach the status of a demonstration, but neither can it be rejected out of hand. Pros and cons should be carefully weighed before any judgment is attempted. A reviewer of my book wrote that there is a "sporting chance" that the Minoan hypothesis is correct.[47] I myself have never put it higher than that.

The reader is referred to my *End of Atlantis* (pp. 46–56, 176–206) for a detailed examination of the Minoan hypothesis. In brief, the argument is that Minoan Crete developed a brilliant and original civilization based on sea power, that this civilization was at its acme around 1475 B.C. when Egyptian horizons were being extended by the conquests of Tuthmosis III, and that a tradition of it, independent of Greek memories of Minos, was formed and preserved in Egypt. The argument requires acceptance of the identification of the "Keftiu" of Egyptian records with "Minoan Crete." It turns further on the likelihood that no classical Greek visitor to Egypt would have associated Keftiu traditions with Crete, partly because of the difference of name, but also because Egyptian antiquarians themselves would have had no clear conception of the location or date of the civilization of Keftiu. "Keftiu" disappears from Egyptian records after about 1400 B.C. One has, therefore, to consider what impression Minoan Crete is likely to have made on the Egyptians in the earlier part of the New Kingdom period. I pointed out that a still extant stele of Tuthmosis III from Karnak helps us to frame an answer to that question. The inscription consists of a Victory Hymn in which Tuthmosis is represented as ruler of the whole world, with Keftiu as an island power at the western limits of that world. I also pointed out that Keftiu is probably derived from a root meaning "pillar," and that a western island containing a "sky-pillar," that is, a lofty mountain helping to support the dome of the sky, would fit neatly into the frame of Bronze Age Egyptian cosmology.

The culminating step in the argument is to suppose that an Egyptian priest took Solon (or, as I now prefer to think, Plato) through a document like the Victory Hymn, and that the Greek associated Keftiu with his own mythology of Atlas. Such an association would be crystallized by the "translation" of Keftiu as "Island of Atlas," for which the Greek is *Atlantis*. Once this "translation" was made it would entail the transference of the legendary island power to the *Greek* "far west," and Plato's placing of Atlantis outside the Pillars of Heracles (Strait of Gibraltar) would follow inevitably.

Frost's original Minoan hypothesis allowed the positing of a documented historical tradition at the heart of the Atlantis legend. This tradition, though much garbled in the course of transmission, was centered in Egypt, the only place where Bronze Age records were accessible to Greeks of the classical period. If the Atlantis legend really originated in Egypt, as Plato says it did, this would help to account for the aura of "history" which so many readers have sensed in it.

Further confirmation of this way of viewing the legend depends on a point by point comparison of Plato's picture of Atlantis with the realities of Minoan civilization as revealed by archaeology in this century. The reader is again referred to my previous study for details (pp. 181-184). Here I will only recall that the kings of Atlantis were from time to time required to enter the precinct of the temple of Poseidon to hunt bulls "without weapons, but with staves and nooses" (*Critias* 119d–e). This detail reminds one very forcibly of the bull games of the Minoan civilization. I have not come across any convincing alternative suggestion of a cultural model from which Plato might have drawn it. My overall conclusion, which I see no reason to modify, was that "it is probably easier to believe that Plato was utilizing a genuine tradition of the topography and customs of Crete, than to suppose that all the parallels are the result of mere coincidence" (p. 183).

This method of identification by an accumulation of circumstantial detail was also initiated by Frost, but there was one respect in which his analysis was less than convincing. He gave no satisfactory explanation of the sudden disappearance of Atlantis "in a single day and night of misfortune" (*Timaeus* 25c–d). A remedy for this defect appeared with the publication in 1939 of an epoch-making paper by Professor Marinatos.[48] Marinatos argued that the power of the Minoans had been seriously weakened by a sudden and violent volcanic eruption on the island of Thera (Santorini). In particular he suggested, on the analogy of the Krakatoa eruption of A.D. 1883, that Crete and Cyclades must have been devastated by seismic sea-waves (tsunamis) caused by the eruption. As long ago as 1885 A. Nicaise had equated Thera with "lost" Atlantis. This suggestion made no impact at the time, but has recently been revived with a wealth of detail by J. Mavor, and A. G. Galanopoulos and E. Bacon.[49] It has received added impetus from the discovery and excavation on the south coast of Thera of a substantial town buried under the eruption debris and showing many Minoan features. In my opinion, to identify Thera with Atlantis *tout court* is to give too definite a geographical solution for what is properly a problem in source criticism. I incline to the view that memories of the zenith *and decline* of Minoan civilization were an important formative element in the Atlantis legend, but this does not commit me to pinpointing the metropolis of Atlantis in pre-eruption Thera.

The problem of the sudden decline of Minoan power can, of course, be discussed without any reference to the legend of Atlantis. Historians have been understandably reluctant to attribute it to a natural cataclysm, but other explanations such as civil war or invasion do not, it seems to me, account so well for the horizon of destruction revealed by the excavation of Minoan sites. Besides the palaces at Mallia, Phaistos, and Zakro, thriving towns at Amnisos, Gournia, Pseira, Mochlos, and Palaikastro were all destroyed and abandoned at a date about 1475–1450 B.C. The assemblages of pottery and other artifacts found in the ruins indicate that the various destructions occurred more or less simultaneously.[50]

I have reviewed the evidence and discussed alternative theories in a recent article.[51] A scientific congress on the Thera volcano was held in 1969, and the papers read on that occasion have contributed substantially to a better understanding of the Bronze Age eruption.[52] In particular, the effects of ash fallout on the eastern half of Crete can now be more realistically assessed. The recent discovery by Charles and Dorothy Vitaliano of traces of ash still persisting in the soil of Crete has, in my view, strengthened the hypothesis that Theran vulcanism was a major factor in the collapse of Minoan civilization.[53]

These various lines of inquiry may seem to take us very far from Atlantis, but if it can be established that a volcanic eruption did indeed wreck the fabric of Minoan culture, we shall at least have to concede that Plato's theory of periodic cataclysms is not without some justification. In this case, there is reason to suppose that the combined action of "fire and flood" undermined the fragile structure of the Minoan thalassocracy and left it vulnerable to a takeover by the Mycenaeans. Such a strange event could hardly fail, we might imagine, to have left some imprint on the traditions of eastern Mediterranean lands. I have elsewhere discussed possible "memories" of the Thera eruption in Greek legend and literature (*The End of Atlantis,* pp. 118–37, 138–41, 145–72). There is also the possibility that an Egyptian notice of its tsunamis may survive in a fragment of Manetho (*The End of Atlantis,* p. 144). The fragment dates "Deucalion's flood" to the reign of "Misphragmuthosis" (probably to be identified with Tuthmosis III, 1490–1436 B.C.). Since the Thera eruption falls within these dates, it is certainly not out of the question to suppose that the fragment contains a garbled reference to the catastrophic rainstorms and tidal waves generated by it. Admittedly, the fragment does not say that Keftiu was destroyed in the "flood." Nor does any Egyptian document now extant say anything about the "end" of Keftiu. But we cannot exclude the possibility that fuller documentation on this matter was available to Solon or Plato.

Though an advocate of the Minoan hypothesis, I would never claim that it explains all the details of the legend of Atlantis. It does, however, provide a basis in history for Frutiger's two essential traits: the power of a "western" island thalassocracy, and the sudden "disappearance" of the island through natural causes. That is its main strength.

Given Plato's normal methods of composition, one would expect to find traits drawn from a number of other sources. Bidez has made a good case for some "oriental" influence.[54] The description of the metropolis of Atlantis is somewhat reminiscent of Herodotus' pictures of Ecbatana and Babylon.[55] The elaborate nature of the irrigation system points in the same direction (*Critias* 118b–e). Plato is probably signalling his debt to Egypt or Babylonia when he attributes a "barbaric appearance" to the vast temple of Poseidon (*Critias* 116d). But Atlantis is not simply the Orient transposed to the West. The picture also contains some recognizably "Libyan" features. The elephants of Atlantis point to Africa (*Critias* 114e). It also seems likely that the circular basins where the Atlantean "triremes" were moored are derived from the *cothons* of Carthage.[56]

Various attempts have been made to find a source for the war between Athens and Atlantis in Greek folktale or saga. Gomperz took seriously the statement of the Platonic scholiast that an embroidered robe depicting scenes from the war was offered to Athena at the Lesser Panathenaea. Clearly, however, the scholion is no more than a misunderstanding of Proclus' metaphorical description of Plato's narrative as an ornamented robe fit for the goddess.[57] Brandenstein supposed that Plato was using a saga going back to the Athens of the Mycenaean Age.[58] E. D. Phillips emphasized the widespread disturbances which brought down the great powers at the end of the Bronze Age, and of which the Great Sea Raid on Egypt was one aspect. He thinks that these events "must have left popular traditions of gigantic wars and invasions in all parts of the eastern Mediterranean." These traditions will have survived in Attica and, conflated with stories of earlier Attic resistance to Minos, have formed part of "a mixed Attic tradition as handed down to Solon."[59]

I do not myself believe that there was any popular Greek basis for Plato's tale. It has some affinities with mythological motifs like the "Golden Age" and the "Isles of the Blest," but such motifs are too generalized to count as sources. Plato, however, may have derived some inspiration from a fifth-century literary presentation of popular mythology. I refer to the work of Hellanicus of Lesbos, whose writings, so far as I am aware, have not previously been discussed in relation to Atlantis criticism. This is all the more surprising given the fact that Hellanicus was the author of works entitled *Phoronis, Deucalioneia,* and *Atlantis* (or *Atlantika,* or *Atlantias*), and that Plato alludes explicitly to the legends of Phoroneus and Deucalion in his introduction of the Atlantis story (*Timaeus* 22a). According to Lesky, Hellanicus aimed at closing the gap between myth and historical tradition in the modern sense.[60] Jacoby also regards him as much more than a mere compiler and speaks highly of his systematic treatment of the early legends.[61] Like Hecataeus, he tried to introduce some rational order into the confused deposit of Greek myth and heroic legend. I have contended that Plato continued the same enterprise, and, if so, it would be natural for him to take some account of Hellanicus' work. In the genealogy of the kings of Atlantis Plato is certainly writing in the manner of Hellanicus, and there may be a more specific debt to be traced. "Atlantis" as used by Hellanicus meant "daughter of Atlas," and the work seems to have been basically a genealogical one.[62] Only a few fragments survive, and one of these recounts how "Poseidon mated with Kelaino and their son Lykos was settled by his father in the isles of the blest."[63] This fragment bears a marked similarity to the account in the *Critias* (113d–e) of Poseidon's mating with Cleito and the island sanctuary fashioned by the god for their offspring.

In general, one should avoid any tendency to restrict Plato's inspiration to one source or one model only. Let me illustrate mythopoeic method, as I conceive it, by an analysis of the theme of the submersion of Atlantis by earthquake and flood. It is instructive to see how Plato handles this, fitting it like a many-sided *tessera* into his mosaic. On one side it is related to some geographical data (invalid, but believed by Plato's contemporaries) about shoal water in the Atlantic.[64] The shoals are neatly explained as the debris of the foundered island. In stressing the suddenness of the disaster—"in one grim day and night"—Plato may well have had in mind the submersion of Helike, Boura, and Aigeira in the Gulf of Corinth in 373 B.C.[65] It was possible, as he knew from an event in his own lifetime, for whole communities to be obliterated overnight by terrestrial upheavals. Yet, from another point of view, the Atlantis disaster is part of his wider scheme of mankind's past as punctuated by catastrophes, a scheme which may have received some confirmation in his mind from Egyptian sources. As a result of the cataclysm "all the fighting men of Athens *en masse* (*athroon*) sank below the ground" (*Timaeus* 25d). Did Plato here have in mind Pindar's description of the ancient war between Zeus and Poseidon when Poseidon plunged "a land and a whole host" (*straton athroon*) down to Tartarus?[66] The epithet *athroon* might be a literary reminiscence of the Pindaric Paean. The background to Pindar's myth is a local Kean tradition that derives ultimately from the Bronze Age Minoan occupation of the island and may contain a memory of the Thera eruption and its effects on the islands of the Aegean. Even if Plato had Pindar's poem in mind, he could hardly have appreciated all its historical roots. But in relation to the theme of cataclysms he may have regarded it as yet another thread in the tangled web of early legend, which was suspended, as he dimly discerned, from at least some historical pegs.

A similar multilevel analysis could be applied to other portions of the Atlantis narrative. Plato's method consists in accumulating materials rather than fabricating them. He constructs his account from the resources of a well-stocked mind, not an erratic imagination. He weaves together and embroiders hints and suggestions from literature, from the past as presented in myth and legend, and from his own experience. As befitted a descendant of Solon, he was, in the phrase he applied to his uncle Charmides, "at once a poet and a philosopher" (*Charmides* 155a). Gifted with remarkable powers of synoptic vision, he could detect connections and patterns in the most diverse and disordered materials. To a mind like his the disaster to Atlantis was both "what did happen" (*ha egeneto*) and "what could happen" (*hoia an genoito*). The analytic mind of Aristotle distinguished more firmly between "events" and "possibilities," requiring the historian to record the former and the poet to handle the latter. In Plato's work the functions of historian and poet were not so sharply differentiated. In composing the great final myth of the *Phaedo* he poeticized the geography and cosmology of his day. In composing the Atlantis story he dramatized beliefs about the remote past. To poeticize science is to transmute fact into symbol. To dramatize history is to invest what is transient with a more enduring significance. Both activities involve that transcendence of the normal antithesis between fact and fiction of which I spoke at the start of this essay.

Many of those who begin by calling Atlantis a fiction end up finding deeper levels of truth in the story. For Stewart the Atlantis myth "reflects, in the form of invaders coming from the West, Plato's hopes and fears as he looks towards the East." For Friedländer, Plato's Ur-Athens is an Athens infused with the Eidos while Atlantis represents an "ideated Orient." Vidal-Naquet conceives the struggle of Athens against Atlantis as a contest between the City of the Same and the City of the Boundless—in effect a revival of the old Neoplatonist concept of the war as an allegory of a cosmic struggle inherent in the nature of the universe.[67]

The richness of the text is such that these three interpretations are not necessarily inconsistent with one another. One of them, or a combination of them, may represent the major lesson that Plato intends to convey. There is probably some truth also in Vidal-

Naquet's subtle thesis (which overlaps the interpretation mentioned in the previous paragraph) that "Athens" and "Atlantis" represent the good and bad destinies of Plato's own native city as he conceived them. "Good" Athens would be a nonmaritime state of hardworking farmers and public-spirited landowners and "bad" Athens would be a maritime state of shifty sailors and covetous merchants.[68]

My own investigation has not been concerned with the problem of the ultimate meaning or moral of the legend. I have aimed rather at showing what sort of materials were available to Plato and how he handled them. I have shown how he operates partly as a historian, following Herodotus in his attitude to Egyptian antiquities, and teasing out the historical implications of Greek myths. Nor does he disdain the epic manner. There are some consciously Homeric touches in the narrative, notably the invocation of Memory and the Muses at the start of Critias' narrative (108c–d) and the Council called by Zeus where the text breaks off (121b–c). In a sense the Atlantis legend is a prose rhapsody, and Plato's Muse knows how to sing "what is like the truth." But, in general, the composition is too matter of fact and morally pointed to rank as poetry. In the end I fall back on the Greek term "myth fashioner" (*muthologos, muthopoios*) as the most appropriate label for Plato here, and I use it in the Greek way. To adapt a famous phrase of Aristotle, a "myth fashioner" is "a kind of historian."[69] He garners traditions and systematizes them. His aim is to evoke the past and to present it in vivid and meaningful detail to his contemporaries. Plato's Atlantis narrative, in my view, constitutes just such an evocation.

Appendix

The Identity of the Narrator of the Critias

Future discussion of this problem will find its starting point in the painstaking analysis of J. K. Davies in his *Athenian Propertied Families 600-300 B.C.* (London, 1971), pp. 322-335. Davies assembles and discusses all the relevant testimonia on the Dropides-Critias family tree, including the important inscriptional evidence for a Critias son of Leaides which was not available before 1949 (*Hesperia,* Suppl. 8 (1949), 399, No. 12). On this basis he is able to construct a stemma linking Dropides I, who was archon in 645/4, to Plato, who died in 347 B.C. This gives us one of the longest family lines attested in Athens, as follows:

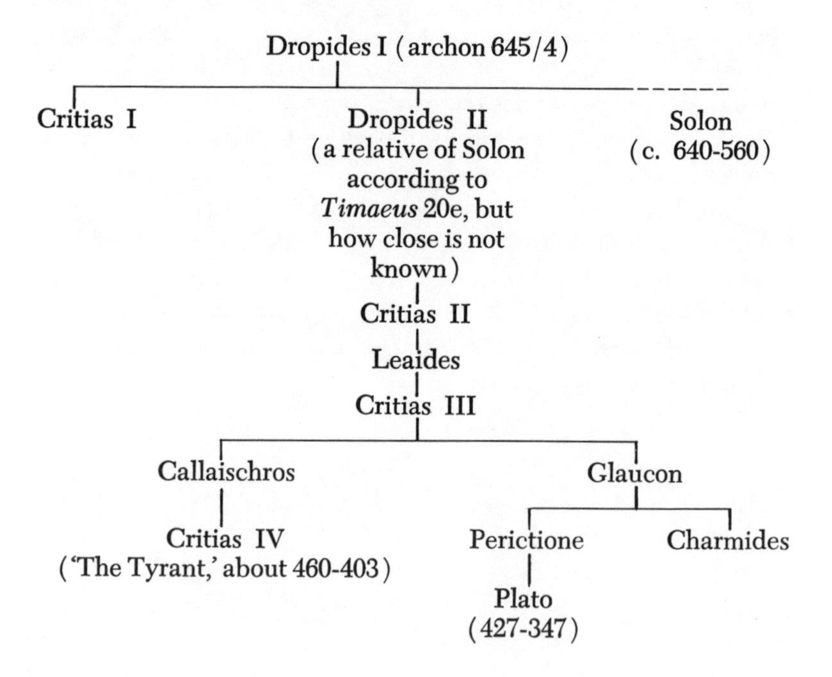

In my *End of Atlantis* (p. 37) I unthinkingly followed Diels and Wilamowitz in assuming that the narrator of the *Critias* must be Critias IV. This is the traditional assumption, but I now see that it is almost certainly incorrect. Burnet was the first to argue that the narrator is to be identified with Critias III, grandfather of the "tyrant" and great-grandfather of Plato (*Greek Philosophy, Part I. Thales to Plato* [London, 1928], p. 338). He was followed by Taylor (*Commentary on the Timaeus*, p. 23), who remarks that this view "fits in with the genealogical facts mentioned" in the *Timaeus*. The passage in question (20e) runs: (Critias is the speaker) "Solon was a relative and close friend of my great-grandfather Dropides [= Dropides II], as he often remarks in his poetry. He told my grandfather [= Critias II], as the old man informed me. . . ."

As Taylor says, "if the speaker were the 'oligarch', we should have to suppose that he has left out two generations of his own ancestors!" It is obviously far more satisfactory to suppose that the speaker is Critias III, whose existence is now independently attested by the inscription mentioned above. We learn from the inscription that he was a candidate for ostracism in the 480s. This implies some prominence as a politician and fits in with Plato's description of him as a figure well-known in Athenian public life (*Timaeus* 20a). He is probably the Critias referred to by Aristotle (*Rhetoric* 1416b.26–29) as an Athenian statesman whose name is better known than his deeds. *Pace* Rosenmeyer ("The Family of Critias," *American Journal of Philology* 70 [1949], 405, note 7), this could hardly be said of the "tyrant"!

If the dramatic date of the *Timaeus* is 421 (Taylor, *Commentary on the Timaeus*, p. 17), Critias will by then be a very old man. Burnet is probably right to see an indication of this in Plato's characterization of him as one who "remembers the events of his boyhood quite well but forgets what happened the other day" (*Timaeus* 26b). If we suppose him to have reached 90, like his grandfather (*Timaeus* 21b), his date of birth can be put about 511. His grandfather (Critias II) told him about Atlantis when he was about 10, that is, about 501, and so he in turn gets a date of birth about 591 B.C. This chronology allows Solon (who probably died in 560/59) to overlap Critias II comfortably. It also allows us to identify Critias II with the Critias whom Solon enjoins to listen to his father (fragment 18).

Some minor difficulties remain, as Davies indicates, but they do not seem serious enough to upset the above argument. In regard to the Platonic text, the most acute difficulty is the statement that the poems of Solon were "new" when Critias III sang them as a boy (*Timaeus* 21b). On the chronology just sketched this would be about 500 B.C. An ingenious solution is given by Taylor (*Commentary On the Timaeus,* pp. 23–24), who argues that the poems of Solon would have been suppressed under the Peisistratids and would have been revived as a novelty under the Cleisthenic democracy. Alternatively, one could adopt Linforth's solution, quoted approvingly by Rosenmeyer ("The Family of Critias," 409, note 19) that "new" merely means new in comparison with Hesiod and Homer.

I conclude that the identification of the narrator of the *Critias* with Critias III is almost certainly correct and that there is no serious discrepancy between Plato's statements and the various other pieces of evidence bearing on the Dropides-Critias family tree.

(I wish to acknowledge with gratitude the stimulus I derived in regard to this [and other] Atlantis problems from discussion with Mr. W. Welliver of Bloomington, Indiana. In an unpublished thesis, which he kindly allowed me to read, Mr. Welliver has a particularly good discussion of the Critias identity problem, and I am happy to find myself so much in agreement with his views.)

THE MYTHOLOGICAL PERSPECTIVE

Plato's Atlantis: A Mythologist Looks at Myth

S. CASEY FREDERICKS

Controversy over the fabulous lost kingdom of Atlantis rages on. Yet, for all the apparent disagreement among Atlantists, they also have at least one thing in common: every Atlantis theory inescapably must begin from the assumption that there is a kernel of historical veracity at the heart of the two mythical accounts of the fall of the ancient civilization provided by Plato. Hence, all the theories share a reliance on the obsolete and reductionist theory of myth known as "Euhemerism." L. Sprague de Camp has described this process:[1]

> . . . most Atlantists assure you that all myths are founded upon fact, and then exaggerate the realistic or historical elements in them in order to support their own theories. . . .
>
> Atlantists . . . also like to deny primitive men the power of imagination, so that they can affirm that all myths contain a large element of literal truth. . . .

Euhemerus of Messene, who gave his name to this long-lived theory, was a philosopher of the early third century B.C.[2] In a utopian romance no longer extant he described an imaginary voyage to an uncharted island in the Indian Ocean, and on the basis of what was seen there he purported to explain the origin of the Greek gods: they were once living men, great men, soldiers and kings; after death, because of their exceptional services to mankind, they were worshipped and, with time, promoted in the popular imagination to the level of gods. The beauty of this theory was that it allowed for what the Greeks had long been coming to regard as the paradoxical nature of myths.

Universally recognized as "false stories," myths still possessed an appeal and durability that was indisputable. It was felt that there was something fundamentally "true" about myths, and Euhemerism responded to this intuition by proposing that these false stories do contain a kernel of historical veracity, though buried in a matrix of imaginative distortions. The early Christian writers, among others, adopted the theory for some of their most telling polemics against pagan belief, and from there on it has enjoyed a prestigious career in Western intellectual history.

The theory seems to have reached the height of its popularity in the eighteenth century, only to be superseded by the entire range of universalist explanations of myth which have appeared regularly over the course of the last century. Yet Euhemerism has always maintained some following, though its views seem to diverge further from the mainstream of myth criticism with each decade. It is not found, for example, as a part of contemporary myth theory in better modern treatments of the subject. Since the publication of Frazer's *Golden Bough*, Euhemerism has been studied by theorists as a historical phenomenon, not as a living, possible theory. And though Lord Raglan's contribution to myth theory is questionable at best, he seems to have delivered the final blow to modern attempts to revive the Euhemeristic approach.[3]

The point has already been made that this outlook plays a part in all theories about Atlantis, and this is true of what may be described as the paradigmatic Atlantis hypothesis of our time. This, of course, is the theory linking the volcanic destruction of the

Minoan culture of Thera (between 1500 and 1450 B.C.) and the contemporaneous setback on Crete with the destruction of Plato's island empire in the Atlantic. The idea is elaborated in other essays in this collection and so there is no need to dwell on details here. But it is worth noting that D. B. Vitaliano is explicit about her own Euhemeristic approach, while J. V. Luce is implicitly Euhemeristic when he admits that his argument "starts from the belief that the legend of Atlantis, like other Greek legends, may embody a hard core of historical fact."[4]

I would argue, to the contrary, that there is no "hard core" of fact in this theory at all—only the most wildly supposititious tissue of conjecture. At the risk of repeating what is pointed out both above and below, something must be said about what the Euhemeristic interpretation has done to Plato's narrative.

In the first place, the Thera proponents must face a battery of discrepancies between the Platonic account and the allegedly "real events" at Thera: Plato's island was of huge dimensions (larger than Libya and Asia Minor put together), outside the Pillars of Heracles in the Atlantic Ocean; it and its city were fully ten times larger than any possible dimensions at either Knossos or Thera; nor does Plato's topography illustrate anything more than his typical, overworked geometric interests—as is also the case with the cosmological passages of *Timaeus;*[5] the fabulous destruction of the city took place, by his acount, 9,000 years (and not 900) before his time; the Atlantic isle was totally submerged forever, whereas Thera, or at least half of it, and all of Crete, remain.

In addition, Plato never connects his Atlantis with Crete in any sense,[6] nor is there the slightest mention of a volcano as the cause of the legendary island's destruction. And Plato's description of a city built up of geometrically regular concentric circles alternating strips of land with canals (*Critias* 113c–116c) has no resemblance to Knossos or to any other Minoan site.

Just what is supposed to be left of the original Plato after the Thera proponents finish with their "corrections" of the text? Certainly nothing in Plato's accounts relates explicitly or directly to the volcano theory at all; only by radically *altering* Plato can his two texts be made to correspond here and there to the preformed Thera hypothesis.

Nor does the theory advance our insight into Plato's story in the least; it does not explain Plato, but explains him away. Sadly, this is the fault with Euhemeristic interpretations of other myths, too: they can only explain myths away and never come to grips with the "other worldly" quality so essential to mythical narratives, for it is the alleged imaginative distortions which constitute the really interesting dimension in myths.

A second inadequacy in the Thera hypothesis stems from its alleged connection with archaeological science. The works of the archaeologically oriented who write about Atlantis are as a rule crammed with charts, site maps, brilliant photographs of landscapes and archaeological finds, and chronological tables—but none of this has anything to do with Plato's story. The alleged connection between Thera and Plato's two dialogues is both artificial and unnecessary.[7] What happens again is that the ancient literary text is dissected into fact and fiction, the former category being applied in Procrustean fashion to whatever in the archaeological evidence looks as if it might fit the preconceived theory. Reasonable and cogent only to the extent that Thera is a real prehistoric Minoan site open to honest archaeological exploration, the whole theory falls to pieces in the face of the objection that there is not a single explicit connection of any kind anywhere between Plato's tale and the site on Santorini.

What this amounts to is that the Thera hypothesis, however sophisticated or erudite, is just another Atlantis theory belonging to a long tradition of such theories and no more a final "factual" solution to the problem than any of its predecessors. Atlantis simply is not a typical Greek legend, as the Thera proponents would have us believe. Even if it were a legend, it would have to be an Egyptian one, for according to Plato's accounts the remembrance of Atlantis' collapse was preserved only in Egypt and it was an Egyptian tale that the Greek Solon took home to his native Athens.

So we should not expect Atlantis to be similar to Greek legends at all. This is a major contradiction in the Thera proponents' analysis of the story, because they all appeal to Heinrich Schliemann with Homer's Troy or Arthur Evans with Minoan Crete as precedents for their own contribution to knowledge of Greek legendary prehistory. However, Atlantis simply is not a popular, ubiquitous myth like Troy or Minos, and in all of its long history there is not a single piece of textual evidence independent of Platonic origin. There really is no need, in fact, to assume (for it can only be an assumption) that Atlantis is a "legend" in the technical sense of an imaginative story which has some real historical event as its origin.

Therefore, it is my suggestion that we abandon the theoretical framework of Euhemerism altogether in evaluating Plato's two accounts of the inundation of Atlantis; the story may be viewed more appropriately and more precisely as an echo of earlier myths. This is perhaps the most important point at which a *contemporary* mythological analysis of Atlantis will depart from all earlier modes of interpretation: with the Structuralists and others, we should begin to interpret myths in the context of other myths,[8] not using supposed events in history as an explanation. Many myths are only transformations of earlier myths or mythical conceptions and have their origins only in earlier states or products of the human imagination. Many myths may thus be analyzed only in relation to other myths and not to events in human history. This does not mean that Atlantis is pure fiction or fancy either, as if it is some totally inexplicable product of Plato's imagination, conjured up *ex nihilo*. The underlying mythical inspiration is significant.

But in order to accomplish such a total revision in our attitude toward Plato's myth, we have to adjust our understanding of the history of Greek mythology in accordance with the more modern trends in myth research. This requires that we momentarily turn our attention away from the volcano at Thera, away from Minoan Crete—in fact, far away from the entire Greek world to Bronze Age Mesopotamia.

The influence of ancient Near Eastern myths and mythical conceptions on Greek mythology is now thoroughly accepted by scholars of the stature of G. S. Kirk, T. B. L. Webster, and Cyrus Gordon.[9] More specifically, M. L. West, N. O. Brown, and Peter Walcot have analyzed the divine succession myth recounted in Hesiod's *Theogony* in relation to its precedents in the Babylonian creation epic, *Enuma Elish*, and the Hittite-Hurrian myth of Kumarbi.[10] Joseph Fontenrose in his magnum opus, *Python*, has exhaustively examined the Greek combat-myth, which describes the victory of a god or hero over a dragonlike, monstrous opponent, as part of a much larger Mediterranean mythological pattern.[11]

A number of other motifs fall within this comparative scope: the Mother Goddess in her role of fructifier of the earth, the paradisiac Golden Age, the Underworld, cataclysms as divine punishment for sinful mankind, and parallels like that between Gilgamesh-Enkidu and Achilles-Patroclus.[12] The extensive bibliography recently compiled by Louis Orlin should reinforce the general direction of this trend in research.[13] We now look to Near Eastern myths as forming the general background of Greek mythology, for much of the latter echoes not the prehistory of its own culture, but the mythical stories and ideas of various cultures of the Bronze Age Near East.

Consequently, we have here not a random collection of isolated examples, but a new paradigm for the comparative study of Greek mythology which makes much of the earlier research obsolete. It can even bear directly upon the study of Atlantis: Luce, for example, tries to "Euhemerize" Talos, the bronze giant of Crete who appears in Apollonius of Rhodes' *Argonautica* (4.1537–1764), transforming him into a memory of the Thera volcano as seen erupting by Jason and the other Argonaut heroes in their travels. But Charles Picard sought a precedent for Talos in the Near East and found it in the stone giant Ullikummi, subject of a Hittite-Hurrian tale that is usually called "The Song of Ullikummi."[14]

The general thesis that a substantial portion of Greek mythology is a special development of Near Eastern mythology entails the specific proposition that the Greek version of the flood myth is one illustration of this same general principle—a view that was taken over thirty years ago by Joseph Fontenrose, and which has been reinforced by scholars in the fields of both classical and Near Eastern studies.[15]

No doubt the story of Noah and his flood told in the Old Testament book of Genesis is the most popular and enduring treatment of this theme, but since the first appearance of George Smith's *The Chaldean Account of Genesis* just a century ago (1876) our knowledge of the prebiblical history of flood legends has grown remarkably. Now three prototypes of Noah from older Mesopotamian cultures are known: the Sumerian tale of Ziusudra (somewhat fragmentary), an Akkadian version named from its hero Atrahasis, and the story of Utnapishtim as recorded in the Akkadian epic of Gilgamesh. Like Noah, except for their polytheism,[16] these stories are all folktales in organization, telling of the gods' plans to destroy a mankind which has been found offensive in their eyes. Then one just man is allowed to escape the general deluge in some sort of boat, and after the waters recede this Noah figure is essential to the reestablishment of human civilization, either spiritually as founder of a cult and worship or physically as parent of the revived human race.

What is most significant, however, is that the general features of the Near Eastern myth as outlined are shared by the Greek stories of the universal deluge of mankind, exemplified perfectly in the tale of Deucalion and Pyrrha found in Ovid's *Metamorphoses* (1.313–415) and Apollodorus' *Library* (1.7.2). They too must be regarded as variants of that same Mesopotamian flood tale that led in another direction to the Old Testament legend. On this issue Kirk may safely be said to have the last word when he asserts that "the Greek flood myth is unquestionably derived from the Mesopotamian exemplar by one means or another."[17]

Serious scholars, then, no longer dispute the dependence of the Greek deluge tale, and this obviates a great deal of earlier research which attempted to connect such stories with local floods in

Greece. In addition, all earlier attempts to link the Greek legend of the deluge directly with the biblical version are obsolete. Both Greek and biblical versions are collateral descendants of a popular and widespread Mesopotamian tale which is over two millennia older than either of them.

It is true, however, that in the Greek versions the element of *story* so essential to the folktale-like Mesopotamian and biblical versions is severely curtailed:[18] there is little interest in the Greek about how Deucalion is informed of the impending catastrophe, no detailed concern about the construction or appearance of the boat, no worry about species of animals to accompany the just man on his craft. Instead, the Greek plays up the conceptual and speculative possibility of the myth, focusing on its articulation of the history of mankind into two distinct eras separated by a cataclysmic event. As Kirk would remind us, this transformation of folktale into speculative concept is typical of Greek adaptations of Near Eastern motifs.[19]

The Greek myth of the deluge, then, should not be used for Euhemeristic purposes at all because this borrowed tale need not refer to any real prehistoric event, either of local or universal extent.[20] Yet this is an important point, inasmuch as Atlantists have continually attempted to appeal to fully mythicized versions of flood stories—sometimes Deucalion's, sometimes Noah's—as confirmation of the reality of the Atlantis legend. Cosmas, the sixth-century author of a fanciful *Christian Topography,* is but the earliest known attempt to look at Atlantis as a garbled Greek version of the biblical flood. This seems to have been a particularly popular approach in the nineteenth century, turning up in Ignatius Donnelly's *Atlantis: The Antediluvian World,* a work which is commonly regarded as the modern prototype of Atlantis speculations. And, as might be expected considering the number of other methodological archaisms associated with the theory, this notion turns up commonly in the writings of the Thera proponents.[21]

But this attempted Euhemeristic connection is suggestive: Atlantis and all these various deluge tales like the Greek and biblical do belong together since *Plato's Atlantis is itself a variant of the flood myth,* albeit one that has undergone the conceptualizing and rationalizing process typical in the history of Greek mythology. Atlantists thus have an interpretation of the relationship perfectly the reverse of the truth. When they try to use flood myths as confirmatory documents, they only point the way to a more cogent interpretation of the evidence—that we should start from the flood myths and then proceed to Atlantis, locating the latter as a member of a mythological series. It is the implications of this new perspective on Atlantis that must be clarified at some length in the following pages, beginning with *Timaeus,* since the legend in its entirety is outlined there, but referring to the fleshed-out and expanded, if narratively truncated, version in *Critias* as need arises.

Plato's immediate narrator of the destruction of Atlantis in *Timaeus* is an anonymous Egyptian priest at Saïs who is speaking with the Athenian politician, Solon. What gives the priest away as a fictive character is the overall *Greek* intellectual framework of his story, which is explicitly intended to illustrate a cyclical theory of history found in two other dialogues, *Politicus* and *Laws.* Based on the formulations of the pre-Socratic philosopher, Empedocles, the theory asserts as its model of time an undulating path of alternating growth and decay, with the effects of any half-cycle being negated by the end of still the next half-cycle.[22]

In *Politicus* (268e–274d), the theory is given a highly cosmological rationale and is modelled directly on the myth of the "Five Ages of Man" found in Hesiod's *Works and Days* (106–201). In *Timaeus* (22c), *Critias* (109d), and *Laws* (Book 3 to 679d), the theory is applied to the dimension of man and his civilizations rather than to the cosmos as a whole, and it is involved with periodical terrestrial catastrophes which destroy whole civilizations, leaving to the men who survive the task of building up society afresh. J. A. Stewart was right long ago to refer to this theory as "part of the 'science' of Plato's day."[23] A *Greek* science, besides. Thus there is no need to go outside the context of earlier Greek philosophical speculation to explain Plato's cyclical theory of catastrophe, even though catastrophes sent by the gods do play an important role in earlier Near Eastern mythology. The Greek theory is probably best explained as a conceptualization of the earlier myth.

But because of the role of the priest, some comment is required on the misuse of Egypt by Atlantists, the Thera proponents included. Although it is now known that Egyptian mythology is, in contradistinction to the Mesopotamian, relatively unimportant for its influence on Greek myth[24]—and the possibility of the Greek cyclical cosmology being a direct borrowing from Egypt is out of the question—the ancient Greeks' own view of their relationship to Egypt is something else.

In early Greek thought there was a persistent notion that much of both Greek science and Greek religion originated in some form of "Oriental" wisdom, with the Egyptians being singled out for special favor because of the unmistakable antiquity of their culture. Indeed, even as early as Herodotus (*History* 2.2) there was serious speculation that life itself began in Egypt, and Aristotle (*Meteorologica* 352b.21) speaks of the Egyptians "whom we hold to be the most ancient of mankind." In *Laws* (2.656e), Plato has his speaker give credence to the conviction that the Egyptians had records going back 10,000 years.

In fact, this seems to be the interpretation we are supposed to put on the entire Greek anthropological attitude toward Egypt: that the antiquity of that nation had shocked the normal Greek sensibility, which had been accustomed to numbering its heroic origin from the gods in only a few generations of men, into starting to think on a temporal scale at least ten times that large (hence, the priest's chiding Solon that the "Greeks are all children"; see also Herodotus, *History* 2.143 and Plato, *Theaetetus* 175a–b). In these terms, Greek ethnography of Egypt made a very real contribution to early Greek historiographical speculation.

In light of this Greek intellectual tradition, it is the simpler explanation to regard the entire account of the transmission of the Atlantis tale—from the priests at Saïs, to Solon, to Dropides, then to his son Critias, and in turn to the younger Critias, Plato's narrator—as a fictional imitation of a genealogy, accomplished deftly in the Herodotean manner,[25] a reading that would fit in well with the character Critias, who behaves in *Timaeus* like an aristocratic Athenian traditionalist. There is no need to assume any Egyptian *reality* at all behind the story, contrary to the wild speculations of Atlantists in this regard.

The overarching Greek theory of the rise and collapse of civilizations ascribed to the Egyptian priest must act as the logical framework that determines all specifics in the Atlantis dialogues. The priest, in fact, explicitly states that catastrophes may be local or universal in scope, due to either fire or water—the two being regarded as the greatest causes of destruction, though lesser ones also exist. Further, the priest says, the Athenians remember only *one* deluge, although there were many, of varying extent (*Timaeus* 23b). Only the latest of these, the one the Athenians do remember, was the universal catastrophe by water which is specified by Solon as that of Deucalion and Pyrrha.[26]

Thus Plato's reference to Deucalion's deluge here is inseparable from his theory of human history as a cyclical pattern of the rise and fall of civilizations, for each and every cataclysm, of whatever kind or extent, is a particular instance of the workings of this same universal law. So, too, the destruction of Atlantis (*Timaeus* 25c) falls under this same class logic—for the priest tells the story of its destruction as an instance of this same pattern.[27]

Hence, Atlantis is not *the* traditional flood—Plato certainly does not say that—but along with the traditional one it is an example of recurrent cataclysms which are inflicted on human civilizations. And yet, it remains essential to an understanding of the origin of Atlantis that the flood myth, articulating human history into ante- and post-catastrophic periods, is the basic inspiration for the tale. The significant change that has taken place is that an old myth has been transformed into a philosophical *concept*.

There is one further piece of evidence that the Platonic account was inspired by the deluge myth. This comes at the very end of

Critias, just before the dialogue breaks off. Plato has just gone through a lengthy description of both the topography and polity of Atlantis—and here there is really very little narrative or "story" value—but he finally does return to the "history" of the fabulous kingdom, supposedly with the intention of giving a fully detailed account of its inundation. But all that is left is an intriguing glimpse into the motivation for the catastrophe:

> Zeus, the god of gods, who rules according to law, and is able to see into such things, perceiving that an honourable race [the Atlanteans] was in a woeful plight, and wanting to inflict punishment on them, that they might be chastened and improve, collected all the gods into their most holy habitation which, being placed in the center of the world, beholds all created things. And when he had called them together, he spake as follows: . . . (*Critias* 121b–c; Jowett translation)

This is still another well attested mythical motif—the gods' decision, often in council, to destroy a mankind gone corrupt. Both Kirk and Webster have recognized it as a theme originating in Near Eastern mythology which turns up commonly in the Greek.[28] More importantly, the motif is also correlated closely with the deluge myth in both the Greek and the Near Eastern versions described earlier, where the gods' decision to destroy mankind through flood constitutes an essential part of the story. The combination of the same two motifs in Plato's expanded version of Atlantis—divine punishment and inundation—is simply too remarkable to be sheer coincidence and makes the ultimate inspiration from the deluge myth all the more likely.

But there is yet another dimension to Plato's conceptual reevaluation of the deluge myth beyond its integration in the cyclical cosmology, and this will go far to explain why Atlantis does not look like a traditional myth but as something more "philosophical." Just as the inundation of Atlantis is parallel to the inundation that destroyed the imaginary antediluvian Athenian culture, it is no less analogous to still another catastrophe mentioned explicitly by the Egyptian priest. This is the story of Phaethon, which is in origin a conflagration disaster rather than a flood. People may believe that a young boy drove the chariot of the sun god, went out of control, and nearly burnt up the earth, but Plato's priest insists that the real truth of the matter is astronomical, namely that periodic conflagrations are caused by deviations of heavenly bodies which move about the earth (*Timaeus* 22c–d). Plato uses exactly the same astronomical theory in *Politicus* (270c–d) to reinterpret heavenly portents associated with the legend of Atreus and Thyestes, where it again illustrates a cyclical cosmology.

So let us observe that the argument has come full circle. Plato himself views the old myths of his culture as imaginative distortions of truths better explained by sciences developed in the sixth century and refined in the fifth—the sciences of history, political science (especially utopian speculation), geography, and astronomy being essential to the reevaluation of the old myths. No less than the modern Atlantis proponent, Plato's Egyptian priest is trying to give a quasi-scientific explanation of legends of catastrophe. And this is nothing more or less than an anticipation of Euhemerus' later theory; it is a dimension of *myth theory* as distinct from myth-making.

Sophistication on Plato's part in the area of myth theory should come as no surprise, for rational and scientific methods of interpreting the traditional deities and stories were already old. As early as Hesiod, in his myth of the "Five Ages of Man" mentioned previously, the nonnaïve and implicitly rationalized quality of Greek myth was already clear. With later, pre-Socratic thinkers, Xenophanes in particular, a philosophical critique of the Homeric and Hesiodic conceptions of the traditional gods was a precondition for a more positive description of the nature of deity. Such rational "theology" constituted one of the earliest and most significant of Greek speculative sciences.

The Sophists, however, went one step further and transformed this theological science into an *anthropological* one, emphasizing the social and cultural implications of man's understanding, or misunderstanding, of the traditional beliefs and stories. On the one hand, this resulted in Protagoras' view of "religion primarily as an anthropological fact to be understood in the light of its meaning and function in human civilization and social structure."[29] On the other, there was Prodicus, living in the latter half of the fifth century, who reduced divinities to natural phenomena, especially the heavenly bodies, and was perhaps the first proponent of the nature theory of myth. Werner Jaeger gives credit to both Prodicus and Democritus for explaining gods and religion "largely by the impressions which natural phenomena make upon the human mind."[30] Thus well before Plato there was a recognizable body of Greek theory concerned with explicating the origin and meaning of the old myths, so that Euhemerus' later theory—evaluating myths as a form of "history"—only put a very particular stamp on something that had been developing in Greek culture for well over a century. Jan de Vries actually locates the origin of "Euhemerism" in the broad sense in the Sophists, Prodicus in particular.[31] Likewise, Herodotus and Thucydides manifest an awareness of this intellectual trend to reevaluate traditional stories: Herodotus by treating the legends of Io and the Trojan War as imaginative reflections of prehistoric conflicts between Europe and Asia (*History* 1.1–5); Thucydides by comparing the legends of Minos and the Trojan War with his own contemporary Athens in terms of naval supremacy (*History* 1.1–23).

Plato's own philosophical career seems to have recapitulated these general developments in Greek culture as a whole. His early view of the traditional gods and myths was mainly a negative Xenophanic critique,[32] but this was later subject to much revision. In works of both his middle and his late periods, Plato is no longer willing to reject myth out of hand as simple falsehood, and myths play a central role in many of these dialogues. Along with *Politicus, Timaeus* and *Critias* are a part of his last phase of mythmaking, comprising the historical and scientific myths which are concerned with man's understanding of his past as related to his present condition in the world[33] (but, being penetrated by mythical structures, both the history and science are *fictive*). *Laws*, Book 10, the philosopher's last statement on this question, also allows deity, myth, and religion a positive function in the ideal state.

Consequently, while it is true, as Ludwig Edelstein has observed, that Plato's "myth is not an entirely artificial creation but is set against the background of common Greek mythology and determined by it,"[34] he is certainly not a naïve or primitive mythmaker. Plato is aware of the radical transformation in the understanding of myth already accomplished by his time, and he is willing to apply contemporary rational sciences to reinterpret it; for that matter, *Timaeus* itself may reasonably be viewed as a conceptualized creation story, and there is no question but that this conceptualization is self-conscious on Plato's part.

In *Critias* (109d–110b), too, Plato has his speaker Critias relate what amounts to still another theory of myth, explaining that only the glorious *names* of precatastrophic kings and heroes like Theseus and the other Athenian Cecropidae were handed down orally to later generations, the rest lost as postcatastrophic humanity had to rebuild society in harsh circumstances.

The recognition that Plato is a sophisticated myth theorist will also explain one other pseudo-problem continually raised by Atlantists: the name of the legendary isle. Herodotus offers the oldest reference to the region outside the Pillars of Heracles as the Atlantic Ocean (*History* 1.202), and Plato only echoes him (*Timaeus* 24e). So when he refers to his mythical landscape as "the Atlantic island" (*he Atlantis nesos*: *Timaeus* 25a, 25d; *Critias* 108e; with minor variations in word order at 113c and 113e), there is no question of any meaning or translation except "the Atlantic island" to specify the largest island in the "true ocean," the Atlantic. This obviates Luce's artificial and overly complicated interpretation of "Atlantis" as the Greek interpretation of the Egyptian word for

Crete which was purportedly associated in their mythological and geographical lore with one of the four pillars of Earth, the Egyptian equivalent of the Greek Atlas.[35]

More importantly, however, Plato even provides a "Euhemeristic" interpretation of the name "Atlantis" in *Critias* (114a):

> And he [the god Poseidon] gave names to all of them [his first ten sons], giving to him that was eldest and king this name which both the entire island and the sea took, being named Atlantic, because the name of the first ruler was Atlas.

Thus Plato is really putting a new theoretical construction on the old mythological character Atlas, and it is important in this connection to remember the debt Euhemerus owed to Plato's story when he composed his own romance of a far-off isle whose first rulers possessed the names of famous Greek gods. John Ferguson says specifically that Euhemerus' Panchaia involves "clear echoes of Plato's Atlantis."[36] Paradoxically, then, an analysis of Atlantis must circle back to where it began—with Euhemerus and his theory of myth, which, far from shedding light on Plato's story, was in great part derived from it.

By mentioning Euhemerus' Atlantis-like fable, I have indirectly touched on one final dimension in Plato's story which also relates to Greek myth. I refer to one of the most popular of all Greek mythical conceptions, the Golden Age, so named from its definitive formulation in Hesiod's "Five Ages of Man," although it is again a theme which may be traced back through Near Eastern predecessors (biblical Eden being a collateral relative) to Sumerian origins.[37] In Greek culture, in its conceptualized and rationalized forms, it develops into utopian speculation.[38] Its presence in Atlantis, sharing features of both utopia and myth, reinforces the view that Plato's tale is a conceptual *myth*, and one determined in great part by the earlier Greek mythology. Nor is this unique to Atlantis: allusions to the Golden Age in *Politicus* and *Laws* are both mythical and utopian.[39]

The utopian connection is obvious in the account in *Critias*, the antediluvian Athens being described as an ideal state analogous to that outlined earlier in *Republic* (as is indicated, besides, at the opening of *Timaeus* [17c], which alludes to the earlier dialogue[40]), as well as to those formulated in *Politicus* and *Laws*.[41] Yet even here there are overtones of traditional myths: (1) The story of the city's origin begins with the Olympian gods' "apportionment of the universe";[42] (2) then there is emphasis on the autochthony, that is, the native origin, of the primeval Athenians;[43] (3) finally, we see their closeness, in their aboriginal state, to the gods Athena and Hephaestus (*Critias* 109c; see also *Timaeus* 24d). Kirk has observed that this latter motif in particular was associated with the Golden Age while the loss of paradise was signalled, correspondingly, by increasing human distance from the gods.[44]

Athens' opponent and villain of the piece, Atlantis, is an "anti-utopia." It is, as many commentators have observed, an imaginary Oriental monarchy, "barbaric" in its splendor. Though founded by a divine progenitor, Poseidon, it is ultimately corrupted by its own wealth and power. Perhaps Plato was thinking of the Persian empire, but Atlantis' elephants have suggested Carthage in the West to others. Here again, however, the same three conventional mythical motifs dominate the portrayal (*Critias* 113b-114c): Olympian apportionment of the cosmos, autochthony of the Atlanteans, and their close relationship with their gods and own divine origins in primeval times, followed ultimately by degeneration.

When Plato mentions that "at that time [the origin of Atlantis] neither ships nor sailing were as yet in existence" (*Critias* 113e), he alludes unmistakably to still another motif popularly associated with the Golden Age. In its agrarian simplicity ("soft primitivism") the Golden Age could do without commerce by sea, and the development of navigation was a mark simultaneously of the rise of human avarice and the end of paradise.[45]

There is also a basis for Plato's description of the wonders of Atlantis in Homer's description of the idealized kingdom of Phaeacia in his *Odyssey*[46]—an important point because Luce has tried to Euhemerize this passage, too, saying it contains a folk memory of Atlantean Crete.[47] It does not, because Phaeacia is only a fantasia variation on the Golden Age theme which served Plato as one inspiration for the portrayal in *Critias*.[48] Once again the Atlantists have an interpretation perfectly the reverse of the correct one.

It is true, however, that Phaeacia was, like its more mythical counterparts, a *materialistic* utopia, and so to the philosophically minded Plato it suggested a corrupt society, not a benign one; thus its suitability to prefigure materialistic Atlantis. This is, of course, the central paradox of Atlantis: it is an "antiutopia," and yet it is also a variant of Golden Age and utopian conceptions. And this is what led to certain anomalies in its later history, namely, that later imitators and borrowers always looked upon the fabulous island as a *utopia;* Ferguson, in fact, discusses Euhemerus, Theopompus, and Iambulus as ancient representatives of this phenomenon,[49] but also modern Atlantists right up to the present have looked upon Plato's antiutopia as a utopia or Golden Age. Ironically, the stuffy philosophical utopia of Athens was totally ignored in later ages, justifying L. Sprague de Camp's remark that "Plato would no doubt be astonished to learn that later generations paid almost as much attention to his Atlantis story, which he himself did not think enough of to finish, as to all the rest of his works put together."[50]

In sum, Atlantis is a distant echo of the old flood myth which manifests a rather complex history. First, Plato had recategorized the flood legend along with all other stories of the destruction of civilization and formed a new class, that of "catastrophes." Second, Plato conceived of all these catastrophes as illustrations of a universal pattern of cyclical time, and, third, he thought that contemporary rational sciences could explain their real nature. Fourth, Plato's account of Atlantis cannot be separated from his quasi-Euhemeristic theory of myth which it documents, and, finally, Plato's self-conscious orientation toward the Golden Age reinforces the conclusion that the Atlantis tale is based upon earlier Greek myth. In the face of these determining factors, all modern Atlantis scholarship which believes Plato is describing a real prehistoric event has fallen into the logical fallacy of recapitulating a false ancient theory of myth.

The Thera-Atlantis hypothesis is really what myth critics call a "displacement," a disguising of the original myth—in this case, the original Platonic tale—within a more realistic framework. Here the actual difference is that the Thera hypothesis is more up-to-date in its science than is its Platonic counterpart. Both draw on the imaginative power of an ancient Near Eastern mythical conception, a cataclysm which obliterates totally a highly cultured people (the Minoans and/or Therans in the volcano theory) under mysterious circumstances. Both apply contemporary sciences to function in the area of explanation: geography, astronomy, historiography, geology, and utopian modelling in Plato, archaeology and geology, especially volcanology, in the Thera hypothesis. Both also use a Euhemeristic theory of myth, but here the ancient philosopher comes out better because the theory was new and sophisticated in his day, archaic and naïve in ours. In so many words, the so-called modern scientific interpretation of Atlantis is really a recapitulation and reinforcement of its original structure and function.

In the future Atlantis will be an object of investigation for the comparative mythologist with his interest in the history of myths, their manifold variants and versions, and their creative adaptation to new cultures. It will remain an object for semantic investigation as critics attempt to understand the unrelenting grip of this ancient myth on the modern popular imagination, with over 2,000 books already published. A "Copernican Revolution" in Atlantis studies is long overdue; it is time for the modern imagination to recognize that Atlantis never existed, either in time or in space, and to realize that the actual location of Atlantis all along has been the world of the mind and its most fascinating imaginative product, myth. This universe of the imagination remains the only landscape where exploration, perhaps even further discovery, awaits Atlantists of the future.

THE HISTORICAL PERSPECTIVE

Atlantis and the Minoan Thalassocracy: A Study in Modern Mythopoeism

J. RUFUS FEARS

As a historical question, the problem of Atlantis presents two approaches. The first is an exercise in source criticism. Is Plato's account of Atlantis derived from a valid independent historical tradition, or is it a poetic fancy, an invention of Plato himself? The second is an exercise in the historical use of archaeological evidence. Does the archaeological material, supplemented by any available literary evidence, permit us to conclude the existence of an island-based imperial power in the prehistoric Mediterranean world?

In his stimulating volume *The End of Atlantis,* J. V. Luce has boldly answered both questions in the affirmative. The legend of Atlantis has a solid historical foundation; it preserves nothing less than the story of the imperial might of Minoan Crete in the mid-second millennium B.C. and the sudden and mysterious collapse at its height of the first empire to rule the waves. The fame of its civilization and its naval might were well known to the contemporary Egyptians, who received reliable and fairly detailed information about the nature and extent of the Minoan empire and its sudden collapse about 1470 B.C., overwhelmed by tidal waves caused by cataclysmic volcanic eruptions on Thera. This information was preserved by the Egyptians and was made available to Solon on his visit to Egypt. Without realizing that this material related to Minos of Knossos, Solon assimilated the information and made notes for an epic poem on the theme. This information, in the form that Solon imposed upon it, was transmitted to Plato, either orally or in manuscript form, and was the basis for his account of Atlantis.[1]

With this evocative account, Luce joins a growing list of serious scholars who have accepted and propagated the equation of Atlantis with Minoan Crete and the traditional thalassocracy of Minos. But the whole idea remains a hypothesis which needs further investigation via rigorous source criticism and critical evaluation of the archaeological material. If it will not stand up under such scrutiny, then we must consider it a myth of modern scholarship which should cease to haunt the pages of serious works on Aegean prehistory.

Turning first to the question of literary sources for the story of Atlantis, we might recall that Plato's account is the first reference to the island empire in any extant literature. Atlantis is mentioned by a number of later writers, including Theophrastus, Posidonius, Strabo, Pliny, Plutarch, Longinus, and Proclus. However, none of these writers refers to any valid independent tradition; their source is always the *Timaeus* and the *Critias*. In these dialogues, Plato presents Critias as the narrator of the tale of Atlantis; his source is said to be a family tradition derived from Solon. Solon, the story went, had learned of Atlantis from a priest at Saïs in Egypt, where written records referring to the kingdom of Atlantis were still extant.

Obviously if we could accept an Egyptian origin for the Platonic story of Atlantis it would be an addition of the greatest possible significance to our knowledge of the political history of the preclassical Mediterranean world. It would be a sorely needed bit of muscle to flesh out the bare bones of archaeology; it would be independent literary evidence that before the historical period of

Greece, the Mediterranean or the Atlantic had been the site of a territorial empire, a political structure which exercised dominion over nearby islands and even over parts of Europe and Africa. Unfortunately, the evidence for an Egyptian, a Solonian, or any independent origin for Plato's story of Atlantis is almost nonexistent. Like Homer's wall around the Achaean camp at Troy, Plato's Atlantis might well be a poetic fiction invented by the author. So Aristotle seems to have thought, and so perhaps should we.[2]

Arguments from silence may seem to bulk large in the following discussion of Atlantis as a historical problem. But such must be the case in dealing with the widely held notion that Plato's Atlantis can, in some sense, be equated with Minoan Crete. The proponents of this equation necessitate this approach. They have suspended all normal rules of evidence by totally removing Atlantis, in time and space, from the context in which Plato explicitly placed it; it is the purpose of this essay to return it to that context. Since Plato is our only independent source for the tale, these "Minoans" can move confidently through their Cloud-cuckoo-land of Atlantis, erecting hypotheses at will in a vacuum of silence. Indeed, it is this very silence which presents the difficulty in accepting Atlantis as the remembrance of a historical event.

First, there is the silence of Egyptian records. No extant ancient Egyptian source refers to an insular maritime empire which can be identified with Atlantis or Minoan Crete. Egyptian records of the new kingdom do mention a land called Keftiu as standing in a tributary relationship to Pharaoh, and the equation Keftiu equals Minoan Crete has played an important role in recent attempts to find a historical core in the tale of Atlantis. But the equation is by no means certain.[3] A reference to Keftiu appears first in the *Admonitions of Ipu-Wer*. The manuscript was written in the Nineteenth or Twentieth Dynasty (about 1350-1100 B.C.), but it is possible that the work was composed as early as the First Intermediate Period (about 2190–2052 B.C.). The annals of Thutmose III proclaim that Keftiu stands in awe of Pharaoh, and tribute from

Keftiu is mentioned as late as the reign of Ramses III (1301–1234).[4] Figures labeled as "coming from the shores of Keftiu" appear on frescoes in Theban tombs under Thutmose III (1502–1440) and Amenhotep II (1448–1422). Earlier, figures on the tomb of Senmut, the architect of Hatshepsut (1501–1480), are clearly depicted in Minoan costume and bearing Minoan objects. However, we cannot determine what name was assigned these foreigners. The figures labeled Keftiu in later tombs are increasingly less clearly Minoan in dress, and the vases which they bear include Syrian or Anatolian as well as Minoan forms.

It lies outside this author's competence to enter into the controversy over whether these references to Keftiu do in fact point to Minoan Crete rather than Cilicia. What should be emphasized is that it is quite misleading to write that "Keftiu is almost certainly Minoan Crete. The identification has been challenged, but is now generally accepted" (*The End of Atlantis,* p. 53). It is at least as likely, in some ways more plausible, that Keftiu refers to Cilicia.[5] It is worth noting the extreme scarcity of clearly identified Minoan imports derived from proper excavations in Egypt. In fact, most of the Aegean imports from this period are Helladic, derived from mainland Greek sites. At any rate, Keftiu is never identified as an imperial power; it is a tributary state with which Egyptians trade. Finally, the sparse Egyptian references to Keftiu offer no justification for the view that "the Egyptians . . . received reliable and fairly detailed information about the nature and extent of the Minoan empire and its sudden collapse about 1470 B.C." (*The End of Atlantis,* p. 194). In fact, references to tribute from Keftiu still appear under Ramses II (1301–1234). Even if Keftiu is Minoan Crete, Egyptian records tell us nothing of its catastrophic and sudden disappearance.

In short, Egyptian annals offer no support for the view that Plato's Atlantis is a dim memory of the imperial might of Minoan Crete in the mid-second millennium B.C. The silence of extant Egyptian sources finds its counterpart in extant Greek sources before Plato. The silence of Herodotus and Thucydides on this question is difficult to explain if there had existed in the fifth century, either at Athens or in Egypt, a tradition of the imperial power of Atlantis.

Solon may well have visited Saïs; we cannot know for certain.[6] Herodotus clearly did. We have his explicit testimony both to his visit and to his discussion with the Saïte priests (2.28; 2.130). Herodotus and the priests spoke of many things, of the source of the Nile, of the origin of the Feasts of Lambs, and of the meaning of the Mysteries. However, there is nothing in the narrative of Herodotus which can be construed as a reference to Atlantis. An earlier Athenian victory over the armada of a great imperial power would have been a natural complement to Herodotus' central theme. And since the story would have been known at Athens as well as at Saïs, it is difficult to imagine that it escaped the ken of this most inquisitive of travelers.

Equal weight should be attached to the silence of Thucydides. If we accept Plato's statement that the story of Atlantis was passed down by family tradition to Critias, who made it known to Socrates, then we must also accept the implication that this tale was bruited about in late fifth-century Athens. Yet in his "Archaeology" Thucydides makes no mention of Atlantis (1.2–22). The "Archaeology" is a long digression written to justify Thucydides' statement that the great war between Athens and Sparta was the most significant political movement which the Greek world had ever experienced. His theme, therefore, in this part of his history is the political and material prosperity of early Greece and the question of its ability to undertake any common political action of any major consequence. Thucydides knew of only two imperial powers in the Greek world before the Dorian invasion: the sea empire of Minos, and the dominion of Agamemnon, "Lord over many isles and all Argos." Nowhere does Thucydides mention Atlantis. Had there existed an Athenian historical tradition of the imperial power of Atlantis, it is hard to believe that the probing researches of Thucydides, the Athenian aristocrat, would not have uncovered it or that his keen mind would not have realized its implications.

The silence of Herodotus and Thucydides, in the particular circumstances, would seem an almost conclusive argument against any independent tradition of Atlantis. However, even more can be added. The *Timaeus* and the *Critias* both belong to the last period of Plato's life. An exact dating of either work is not possible, but Plato's death in 347 represents a clear *terminus post quem non* and a clear date by which the Platonic story of Atlantis was known at Athens. In his *Panathenaicus* (189–95), written between 342–339 B.C., Isocrates followed tradition and referred to the ancient exploits of Athens, those deeds of the Athenian forefathers which placed the city in the forefront of the war against the barbarian, generations before Marathon.

In those days of long ago, when the other Hellenic cities had just been founded and Athens was still ruled by kings, Greece was beset by wars. Briefly, Isocrates tells of those enemies who attacked Athens in her earliest period, the Thracians led by Eumolpus, the Scythians led by the Amazons, and the Peloponnesians led by Eurystheus. Plato's attack by the Atlanteans is conspicuously absent, and its absence is not fortuitous. Like Plato, Isocrates had been a companion of Socrates, and he is mentioned warmly in the *Phaedrus* (278); Platonic influence on the *Panathenaicus* has been discerned.[7] One can hardly understand the intellectual climate of Athens and doubt that, at the least, Isocrates knew of Plato's tale of Atlantis, published at a minimum of eight years earlier. His refusal to refer to Atlantis may be taken as evidence that Plato's great contemporary recognized that no historical tradition lay behind the grand story of an Athenian victory over Atlantis.

Furthermore, Isocrates' *Panathenaicus* followed, of necessity, basic conventions required of every such encomium. The public knew what stories properly belonged in a speech praising their forefathers of the Heroic Age, so that the absence of any reference to Atlantis in either the *Panegyricus* or the *Panathenaicus* suggests that no popular tradition existed concerning an Athenian victory over an Atlantean armada. In short, Isocrates shows that Plato's contemporaries knew of no tradition of Atlantis and, further, that they recognized his story of Atlantis for the poetic invention that it was.

In his silence regarding Atlantis, Isocrates is joined by every author of an extant panegyric on Athens, including Plato himself in the curious dialogue *Menexenus.* Particularly noteworthy is the absence of any reference to Atlantis in the *Panathenaicus* (66–73) of Aelius Aristides. Aristides was an avid student of Platonic philosophy and his silence suggests that he realized that the tale of Atlantis had no place in a celebration of the historical glories of Athens. Finally, as the culmination of Panathenaic oratorical tradition, Aristides' *Panathenaicus* again proves that there existed no popular Athenian tradition of Atlantis.[8]

Therefore, in the absence of any evidence from Egyptian sources, the silence of Thucydides, Herodotus, Isocrates, and Aelius Aristides seems conclusive. Plato's story does not reflect a historical tradition derived from Egypt or Solon or from anywhere or anyone else. It is a poetic invention of Plato.

The conclusion is hardly novel. There have been serious students who have taken earnestly Plato's tale of an Egyptian tradition for the story of Atlantis. However, as Professor Luce points out in his essay above (pp. 49–50), for the great Platonists like Cornford and Taylor (and he might have added Ritter and Friedländer) the tradition was simply a fiction of Plato.

Jowett too recognized that attempts to pursue the historicity of Atlantis were devoid of the possibility of any serious results. Such efforts possess an intrinsic interest and a serious lesson only if we remember that "now as formerly the human mind is liable to be imposed upon by the illusions of the past, which are ever assuming some new form."[9]

Thus summarily dismissed from the realm of historical possibility by serious Platonists and source critics, Atlantis as a historical problem would reenter the sober world of classical scholarship by the circuitous route of archaeology. A year before the publication of Jowett's rigorously sensible analysis of the fable of Atlantis, Schliemann began his historic excavations at Troy. For the master of Balliol, Plato's Atlantis was of a piece with Homer's tale of Troy and the romance of Arthur. Schliemann's epoch-making discoveries at Troy and at Mycenae confounded those who regarded the Homeric epic of Troy as legend and nothing more. Bronze Age archaeology became a brave new world for classical scholarship. In subsequent excavations at Tiryns, Iolkos, Thebes, and elsewhere, it was revealed that powerful Bronze Age citadels occupied the sites of those very places featured in the major Greek heroic sagas, and few would doubt that a kernel of historical truth lies at the heart of Greek mythology concerning the Heroic Age.[10]

No less epoch-making than Schliemann's work at Troy and Mycenae were the excavations undertaken by Sir Arthur Evans at Knossos. Directed by Evans over a number of years, the excavations revealed that in the Bronze Age, Knossos had been the site of an extensive palace of complex plan. Excavations elsewhere in Crete uncovered remains of other palaces, villas, and towns. Clearly in the first half of the second millennium B.C., Crete had been the site of an extraordinarily rich and creative pre-Hellenic civilization, which Evans labeled Minoan even as he gave the name Palace of Minos to the great edifice at Knossos. In this matter his terminology has become standard and has formed a framework which still shapes our view of Aegean history in the second millennium. His reasons for the adoption of the term "Minoan" are thus worth quoting:[11]

> The progressive revelations, from 1900 onwards, of a high early civilization on Cretan soil entailed the urgent necessity for devising a new system and terminology for the Late Prehistoric Age in the Aegean area. . . . For the first time there had come into view a primitive European civilization, the earliest phase of which goes back even beyond the days of the First Dynasty of Egypt. To this early civilization of Crete as a whole I have proposed . . . to apply the name "Minoan." By the Greeks themselves the memory of the great Age that had preceded their own diffusion throughout the Aegean lands was summed up in the name of Minos. It is true that very different traditions were connected with that name. On the one side we gain a vision of a beneficent ruler, patron of the

arts, founder of palaces, stablisher of civilized dominion. On the other is depicted a tyrant and destroyer. . . . But the fabulous accounts of the Minotaur and his victims are themselves expressive of a childish wonder at the mighty creations of a civilization beyond the ken of the new-comers. The spade of the excavator has indeed done much to explain and confute them. The ogre's den turns out to be a peaceful abode of priest-kings; in some respects more modern in its equipments than anything produced by classical Greece.

Excavations on the Greek mainland and at the mound of Hissarlik transported from legend into history the Homeric Nestor of sandy Pylos, Agamemnon of wide-streeted Mycenae, and Priam of strong-towered Troy. Evans' genius did the same for Minos of Knossos, bosom friend of Zeus, lord of the sea, proprietor of the Labyrinth, and stepfather of its denizen the Minotaur. Critical nineteenth-century historians thought it pointless to search for valid historical material in the disparate legends which surrounded the figure of Minos, but the excavations at Knossos changed all that.

For enthusiasts, major elements in the story of Minos took on a concrete form. The serpentine character of the ruins of the palace were said to have preserved for later ages the actual name of the Palace of Minos, the Labyrinth—the "Place of the Double Axe." *Labyrinthos*, as we shall see, has been read on a Linear B tablet as presumably a reference to the palace itself. The root of the word has generally been assumed to be *labyrs*, a Lydian word for axe. Certainly the palace at Knossos is preeminently the Place of the Double Axe, an object which appears frequently on the stone blocks of the palace walls, on sacred pillars, and on objects found within the palace.

Like the *-inthos* suffix in *labyrinthos*, the root *labyrs* and the double axe as a cult object point to the southern coast of Asia Minor, an area linked by Herodotus to pre-Hellenic Crete and to Minos of Knossos. The institution of sacral kingship has been thought to be reflected in the tradition that Minos was the bosom friend (*oaristes*) of Zeus. This too has been thought to receive archaeological confirmation in the palace shrines at Knossos and elsewhere. Even the Minotaur has emerged into the light of history; the grim tale has been seen as a dim remembrance of the famous bull games held in the very courtyard of the palace.

Tradition knew Minos as more than merely lord over Knossos. As early as Herodotus, he was seen as the first known figure to exercise dominion over the sea. He was the first person known from tradition to have established a navy, and with his navy, Herodotus tells us (1.171; 3.122), he made himself master of the Aegean and ruled over and colonized the Cyclades. For Thucydides (1.4–8) this thalassocracy of Minos was the first political fact in Greek history. As with the Labyrinth and the Minotaur, the archaeological evidence has been thought to confirm this tradition of the imperial might of Minos.[12] By the Late Minoan I period (about 1500 B.C.) there existed on Crete a regular network of roads, with guard stations at regular intervals, pointing to a centralized power ruling over all Crete. The impression of Cretan unity is further suggested by the close similarity of building materials and ceramic styles all over the island.

Even more importance has been attached to the presence of Minoan artifacts throughout the eastern Mediterranean. Middle Minoan II-III pottery (about 1850–1500 B.C.) has been found throughout the Cyclades, on Keos, Delos, Thera, Naxos, Aegina, Kythera, Paros, and Amorgos. Loom weights with one or two perforations, identical in size to those found at Gournia, have been discovered on Delos, Thera, and Keos. Frescoes showing the clear stylistic influence of Crete have been excavated at Phylakopi on Melos, on Thera, and on Keos, where Minoan architectural elements as well as Minoan pottery and other imports have been taken as evidence of colonists from Crete. Keos has also yielded evidence of Linear A script. Indeed, this Minoan material from Keos is of particular interest in light of the ancient tradition that Minos visited this island with an army in fifty ships and, having wed Dexithea, departed, leaving half of his warriors with her.[13]

Minoan influence is not confined to the Cyclades in Middle

Minoan II–III and Late Minoan I. A settlement at Trianda on Rhodes has no previous history and the pottery includes Minoan domestic ware, strongly indicating an actual settlement of Cretans. Particularly in the Middle Minoan II period (about 1850–1750 B.C.), Crete seems to have had fairly extensive relations with Syria and Egypt. Minoan pottery has been found at Byblos, Ras Shamra, and at Abydos. As was noted, Minoan objects have been recognized in tomb paintings of the Eighteenth Dynasty, under Hatshepsut, Thutmose III, and early in the reign of Amenhotep II.

Beginning slightly earlier but extending well into the fifteenth century is the great age of Minoan cultural influence on the Greek mainland, best exemplified in the material from the shaft graves at Mycenae. Even the western Mediterranean has been thought to bear witness to Minoan cultural influence. A strong folklore tradition linked Minos with Sicily, and Minoan objects have frequently been reported in Sicily and in Italy.

Since Evans there has been a consistent tendency to link this evidence of Minoan cultural influence with the literary tradition of the thalassocracy of Minos. In this view, in the mid-second millennium Crete ruled the waves, exercising political and economic dominion throughout the Aegean by means of her fleet and colonial settlements. J. D. S. Pendlebury gives the most graphic account of the Minoan empire in this period:

> Crete in the sixteenth century became a world power. That she is not mentioned as such in contemporary Egyptian documents must be due solely to the fact that she was in peaceful relationship with that country. Her warlike exploits were confined to the expansion of her empire to the North, over the Mainland and Islands, and according to legend westwards to Sicily. The acquisition of that empire probably began in very much the same way as the British Empire in India. First of all, come the trading stations. All over the Aegean the name Minoa survived into historical times. . . . These may have been the names given by the original inhabitants to the station occupied by the traders of Minos or by the traders themselves. The next stage is when a local prince calls on the traders for help against a neighbor, which is given at a price. And

so, gradually and probably peacefully, most of the country comes under the power of the newcomers. Finally comes the stage when further acquisitions become necessary owing to the need of putting down piracy or rather of ensuring against other seafarers poaching on their preserves. The peace of the seas is essential to an empire whose wealth is based on trade, and the thalassocracy of Minos is no myth.[14]

For Pendlebury and many others, the Minoan thalassocracy was a reality, attested to by the archaeological evidence of Cretan cultural influence and corroborated by Greek literary tradition concerning Minos.[15] At the very height came the crash. Minoan power terminated in a sudden and widespread but mysterious disaster. As Evans reconstructed it, around 1400 B.C. the palace at Knossos was destroyed by fire and systematically looted. The same destruction accompanied by looting occurred at the same time at a number of sites throughout Crete.

It was perhaps inevitable that the theme of Atlantis would be drawn into this portrait of a Cretan thalassocracy and its mysterious disappearance. As early as 1909, K. T. Frost sought to link Atlantis to the brave new world emerging from Evans' excavations on Crete:

The recent excavations in Crete have made it necessary to reconsider the whole scheme of Mediterranean history before the classical period. . . . It has been established beyond any doubt that, during the rule of the 18th Dynasty in Egypt, . . . Crete was the centre of a great empire whose trade and influence extended from the North Adriatic to Tel el Amarna and from Sicily to Syria. The whole seaborne trade between Europe, Asia, and Africa was in Cretan hands, and the legends of Theseus seem to show that the Minoans dominated the Greek islands and the coasts of Africa. . . . The Minoan realm, therefore, was a vast and ancient power which was united by the same sea which divided it from other nations, so that it seemed to be a separate continent with a genius of its own. . . . As a political and commercial force, therefore, Knossos and its allied cities were swept away just when they seemed strongest and safest. It was as if the whole kingdom had sunk in the sea, as if the tale of Atlantis were true. The parallel is not fortuitous. If the account of Atlantis be compared with the history of Crete and her relationship with Greece and Egypt, it seems almost certain that here we have an echo of the Minoans.[16]

So argued K. T. Frost, and since his original article in 1909 there has been a recurrent and understandable tendency to link the myth of the island empire of Atlantis and its disappearance under the sea with that of the Minoan thalassocracy and the sudden destruction of Knossos. Major additional support for the equation of Minoan Crete with Atlantis has been sought in research into the effects of the volcanic eruption of Thera sometime around 1500–1450 B.C.[17] According to the distinguished Greek archaeologist Marinatos, the sudden collapse of Minoan civilization was the result of a natural catastrophe of unparalleled violence, the shock waves and gigantic tidal waves generated by the eruption of Thera. The heartland of the Minoan empire together with the Minoanized archipelago surrounding Thera foundered under the savage impact of the eruption, tidal waves, and ash fallout, which crippled the social, economic, and political life of Crete and paved the way for the Aegean to pass from Minoan to Mycenaean hegemony. Here is the historical kernel of the tale of Atlantis. Here is the grim historical reality behind Plato's words: "But afterwards there occurred violent earthquakes and floods, and in a single day and night of misfortune the island of Atlantis disappeared in the depths of the sea" (*Timaeus* 27d).

J. V. Luce's *The End of Atlantis* provides the fullest statement of this view of the end of Minoan civilization and of its equation with the tale of Atlantis. However, despite the popular appeal of these latter-day Euhemerists, this elaborate picture equating Atlantis with Minoan Crete is a phantasm. It is a Platonic myth built upon what could easily be a myth of modern archaeology—the idea of a pre-Hellenic Cretan thalassocracy. Common and essential to every equation of Minoan Crete with Atlantis is the assumption that pre-Hellenic Crete was the site of an island-based imperial power, possessing a powerful navy, controlling the sea lanes, and exercising dominion over the Cyclades and part of the mainland. It is a view which, since Evans formulated it, has held wide acceptance, and it is a theory of remarkable resilience. It has survived the decipherment of the Linear B tablets at Knossos and the resultant recognition that Greeks occupied Knossos in the Late Minoan II period, the apogee of the Minoan empire in the view of Evans and Pendlebury. For post-Ventris champions of Minoan seapower the grand age of the Minoan Peace has been removed in time to the period between 1950–1550 B.C., the Middle Minoan period; but the assumptions on which this image of a Minoan thalassocracy are based remain the same as for Evans and Pendlebury.

Briefly put, the concept of a Minoan thalassocracy rests upon four assumptions: (1) the presence of Minoan artifacts and other indications of Minoan cultural influence outside Crete implies Minoan political domination and a Minoan commercial and military fleet to transport the items and to provide for safe transport; (2) the scarcity of fortifications on Crete in this period implies Minoan control of the sea; (3) the widespread occurrence of Minoa as a place name in the Mediterranean reflects the period of Minoan imperial and economic control; and (4) the literary tradition of Minos the thalassocrat corroborates the archaeological evidence in proving the existence of a pre-Hellenic Cretan thalassocracy.

Unfortunately, none of this can be proved. In the first place, the archaeological evidence for Minoan cultural influence throughout the Aegean cannot be used to support the view that in the same period Minoan Crete exercised political or commercial dominion throughout the Aegean. To some extent, the prevalence of Minoan artifacts in the Mediterranean world during the middle of the second millennium tends to be exaggerated, particularly in general accounts.[18] In Egypt, for example, only one Late Minoan I painted vase is definitely known, and no Late Minoan II ware has been found. On the other hand, a considerable quantity of contemporary mainland Greek ware has been discovered in Egypt.

However, earlier, in the Middle Minoan period, Cretan contacts with Egypt and the Levant were more extensive.

By contrast, the frequent assertion of widespread Minoan trade with Sicily and Italy rests upon no archaeological evidence. Only four genuine Minoan pottery fragments have been found in Italy and the adjacent islands, all four from the Lipari Islands. No certain example of a Minoan vase has been found in Sicily; indeed, nothing of purely Minoan material has yet been discovered. Contact between Sicily and the Aegean was certainly strong from at least 1500 B.C., but all the imported material seems to be Mycenaean. This absence of any archaeological evidence for Minoan contact with Sicily is particularly significant in light of the persistent Greek tradition that Minos died in Sicily.

Beyond all this, a fundamental methodological error vitiates any attempt to substantiate a Minoan thalassocracy on the basis of the disposition of Minoan artifacts. These artifacts are mute; they tell nothing of political history or even of who transported them. The political history and organization of Minoan Crete is, in every sense of the phrase, *terra incognita*. We do not know a single fact of Minoan political history, not the name of a single king or a single political incident. We assume that the palaces imply kingship, but even this is an assumption. In the period of Greek occupation at Knossos in Late Minoan II, the title *wanax* appears on tablets from the palace. This has been rightly taken as a royal title. However, we have nothing similar from the Minoan Age proper which permits us with certainty to project the institution of monarchy into the political institutions of pre-Hellenic Crete. It is worth pointing out that, in contrast to the great monarchies of Egypt and the ancient Near East, the royal image does not dominate the art of Minoan Crete. There is nothing from Minoan Crete which in any sense equals the unequivocal statement of monarchy found on such objects as the Narmer Palette from the earliest dynastic period of Egypt or on the Vultures Stele from early Sumer.

However, whatever may be the evidence for monarchy in

Minoan Crete, it remains a fact that we must reconstruct the political history of Minoan Crete entirely from the material remains and without the aid of a skeletal framework of political history or even a single reference to Crete as a political power in contemporary Egyptian or Near Eastern records.

Already Thucydides recognized how misleading can be any attempt to determine the political or military strength of a nation on the basis of its material remains (1.10). Furthermore, we possess a clear parallel which should caution us against building any theories of Minoan imperial or commercial domination upon evidence supplied entirely from the disposition of artifacts. I refer to the course of colonization and trade in archaic Greece and Italy of the eighth through the sixth centuries B.C. Beginning in the second half of the eighth century, Greek wares were imported in ever increasing amounts into the cities of Etruria. A Greek script came to be employed for the Etruscan language; painting and sculpture came to be so strongly Hellenized that in many respects Etruscan art in this period can be viewed as a provincial offshoot of Greek art. Even in religion, that aspect of its culture in which a people tends to be most conservative, the Etruscans came under Hellenic influence, building houses for their gods in Greek fashion, representing the divinities in anthropomorphic form in the manner of the Greeks, and even adopting Greek deities such as Apollo and Heracles.

Yet we know in this instance from literary sources that there was no Greek political domination of the Etruscan cities. Cultural influence was the result of individual merchants and of immigrant Greek artisans. Based on this obvious parallel, the presence of Minoan frescoes, Linear Script A, Minoan loom weights, and imported Minoan pottery and local imitations of Minoan pottery on Thera, Melos, and Keos need not mean Minoan political subjugation, any more than Corinthian pottery at Tarquinii implies Corinthian political control.

Colonization is no sure indication of imperial pretensions on the part of the mother country any more than cultural influence is.

Even if it should be clearly ascertained that Cretans established a colony at Trianda on Rhodes, this would prove nothing concerning a Minoan thalassocracy. In the archaic period, Greek colonies were established in southern Italy and in Sicily. There Greek colonies are not evidence of the imperial pretensions of the mother cities. Quite the contrary, the colonies were completely autonomous, bound to the mother city only by sentimental ties. Can we assume that the ties of the Bronze Age Cretans on Rhodes were closer to Knossos or any Cretan political power?

A final objection should be raised against another presupposition which has permitted the deduction of a Minoan Cretan thalassocracy from the disposition of Minoan artifacts in the Aegean. Bluntly put, we do not know who transported Minoan objects to the Cyclades, the Levant, and Egypt. The presence of Minoan artifacts does not imply control of the sea by the Minoans or, even necessarily, a Minoan merchant fleet. Certainly neither the Corinthians nor the Athenians controlled the Mediterranean in the seventh and sixth centuries B.C., yet the pottery of first the one, then the other dominated the market.

The case of Carthage offers a classic example that the presence or absence of artifacts gives no secure evidence for the maritime strength of any state. In the classical period, Carthage was the Mediterranean state in which commerce played the greatest part. Beginning in the late sixth century B.C., Carthage sought to enforce the policy of a closed sea in the western Mediterranean. Yet if we possessed only the archaeological evidence, we could never deduce the political fact of a Carthaginian thalassocracy. This great trading state and maritime power has left few Carthaginian artifacts, perhaps both because a large part of the trade was in perishable items and because the Carthaginians were middlemen, carrying the produce of other cities.

Thus, critically examined, Minoan cultural influence and the disposition of Minoan artifacts throughout the Aegean do not support the concept of a Minoan thalassocracy as a historical reality. The same is true of the absence of fortifications on Crete and the widespread occurrence of the place name Minoa throughout the Aegean.

The ring wall around the residential area behind the palace at Mallia is exceptional, and the scarcity of fortifications on Minoan sites has frequently been interpreted as evidence that the Cretans controlled the sea and protected their shores by means of a war fleet. The great palaces at Phaistos and Knossos, it is argued, needed no fortifications while Crete stood safe behind her wall of ships. This is not the only or indeed the most likely historical interpretation of the monumental evidence. It is not to be doubted that ships, including long distance merchant ships, existed in Minoan Crete.[19] However, the fleet necessary to enforce a Minoan Peace throughout the Aegean would have been of a far larger order. No such fleet existed in Tutmoside Egypt.[20] The Egyptian fleet functioned largely for troop and freight transport, for trading and exploration, and as a mobile base of operations for expeditions along the Syrian coast and up the Nile. Such a fleet did not rule the waves or even clear the sea of pirates.

The insular nature of Crete should not lead us to assume that the Minoans were more precocious in the adoption of modern naval strategy than the Egyptians. It has been perceptively pointed out that insular states tend to rely upon the sea as a protective moat, to meet invasions at the shore, and not to have navies until experience indicates the necessity to meet outside threats at sea.[21] This is clearly suggested by the naval history of the three major insular powers of modern history, Great Britain, the United States, and Japan. Harold met Harold Hadrada and William on land; the Americans in 1812 met the British invasions on land at Baltimore and New Orleans; the major Japanese resistance to both invasions of Kublai Khan occurred on land. The English, the Americans, and the Japanese all possessed only small naval forces. The point is that these insular states did not instinctively adopt a concept that safety lay in maritime strength.

Under Themistocles' leadership and after the experience of Marathon, early fifth-century Athens did adopt such a naval strategy, and our evidence for the Athenian thalassocracy is ample. For the thalassocracy of Minoan Crete we possess not a single piece of contemporary evidence. There is no extant representation in Minoan art of a naval battle.[22] In these circumstances it is valid to ask whether the concept of control of the sea is not anachronistic when applied to the Mediterranean world in the second millennium B.C. It is significant that the only seaborne invasion from this period known to us in detail was met at the shore. Ramses III drew his warships up at the rivermouths to defend Egypt against the Peoples of the Sea, while stockades were prepared on the shore. The invaders were "dragged in, enclosed, and prostrated on the beach."[23]

In short, we have no evidence that the strategical concepts inherent in the idea of thalassocracy existed in the second millennium B.C. Furthermore, we cannot assume that the Cretans possessed a powerful war fleet because they inhabited an island. In these circumstances, it is wrong to argue that the absence of fortifications proves Minoan control of the sea. The scarcity of fortifications suggests political unity and the absence of internal warfare on Crete. It may also imply that, before the Greek conquest of Knossos, no foreign invader possessed the capability to launch a seaborne invasion of Crete. However, it indicates nothing concerning a Minoan thalassocracy.

In the same way, the occurrence of Minoa as a place name offers no firm evidence for the thalassocracy of Minos.[24] Even antagonists of the theory of a Minoan thalassocracy have found it difficult to circumvent the argument of Evans and others that the place name Minoa had survived from the great age of Minoan sea power down into the historical period. The occurrence of Minoa as a place name throughout the Aegean, it is argued, bears witness to the abiding memory of the Minoan empire, preserving the name and site of trading stations erected in the great age of the Minoan sea empire, when Cretan merchants plied the seas under the protection of the great dynasty at Knossos.

But once again the evidence permits quite a different interpretation. The *Ethnika* of Stephanus of Byzantium (p. 454, ed. Meineke) is the major source for Minoa in Aegean toponymy. The list of Stephanus records eight such Minoas: one on Amorgos, a second in Sicily, a third on Siphnos, a fourth on Crete, a fifth in Arabia, while Gaza, Paros, and an island off the coast of Megara also bore the name. Other geographers permit us to supplement Stephanus' list with the knowledge that there were two towns called Minoa on Crete and that Minoa was also a place name in Laconia.[25] Crete, Amorgos, Paros, Siphnos were clearly in the orbit of Minoan cultural influence, and the possible site of the Minoa near Megara has yielded slight Minoan ceramic evidence.

In no case, however, does the archaeological evidence even suggest that any of these Minoas was a Minoan trading station. Many of the Minoas cannot be exactly located, and only one, Heracleia Minoa, has been systematically excavated.[26] In this case, it is clearly established that the name Minoa is not the survival of a Minoan trading station, for the site has yielded no evidence of Bronze Age habitation. It seems clear that the town was a secondary colony of Selinus founded in the second half of the sixth century B.C. As the other half of its double name indicates, Heracleia Minoa was so dubbed in homage to two great Dorian heroes, Heracles and Minos. Heracleia Minoa was one of thirty sites throughout the Greek world whose names honored Heracles.

This phenomenon points to a basic fallacy in the argument that Minoa as a place name testifies to a Cretan commercial empire. It is consistently assumed that the parallel to these Minoas are the Alexandrias and Caesareas of the ancient world, cities named after the dynast who ruled the territory. Yet as is certainly true for Minoa in Sicily, more likely parallels are Heracleia and Apollonia.[27] No one doubts that Minos, Heracles, and Apollo all exercised a powerful influence on the mentality of the archaic Greek world. One wished to endow the town with the protective charisma inherent in the name of the hero or the divinity. Minoa as a place name testifies to the reputation of the mythical Minos in the archaic and classical period, but it need not suggest that Minos ever ruled the territories which bore his name any more than Heracleia and Apollonia suggest this about Heracles and Apollo.

Finally, it is plausible to argue that originally the place name Minoa had no relation to Minos of Knossos. It is by no means certain that Minos and Minoa are derived from the same root. Several of the escapades of Minos seem clearly etiological in origin, aimed at explaining the presence of the place name Minoa, for example near Megara.[28] It is not out of the question that the place name Minoa, originally unrelated to Minos, gave rise to the view that Minos ruled the sea. The name Minoa might have been explained by linking it to the rule of the famed lawgiver of Knossos, and the presence of Minoas in the Cyclades could have given rise to the idea that Minos had a navy. Otherwise how could he have dominated Paros, Siphnos, and Amorgos and thus have left the evidence of his name? Whatever the origin of Minoa as a place name, it cannot be assumed to be evidence of a Minoan empire or even of Cretan emporia.

I have argued at length that, in the absence of any literary evidence, the evidence of archaeology and toponymy cannot support the concept of a Minoan Cretan thalassocracy. To this, it might be objected that we do possess such literary evidence in the form of the Greek tradition of Minos of Knossos, ruler of the sea. Indeed, since Sir Arthur Evans there has been a consistent tendency to regard the Minos of Greek legend as an indigenous Cretan ruler, master over Knossos at some time during the grand period of Minoan civilization in the seventeenth and sixteenth centuries B.C. This has been done only by ignoring two essential elements in the literary image of Minos—the persistent tradition that Minos was an Achaean, and the persistent chronological framework which placed the rule of Minos two generations before the Trojan War. Both traditions already appear in the *Iliad* (13.445–54), which must form the starting point in any attempt to determine the image of Minos in Greek folk memory. Neither of the two elements in the tradition can be dismissed or ignored. It is now quite clear that by the mid-fifteenth century a Greek dynasty ruled at Knossos. Already suggested by a variety of archaeological evidence, this has been made conclusive by the decipherment of Linear Script B, showing that Greek was the administrative language at Knossos in the last phase of the palace. Homer's Minos, the Greek or Achaean lord of Knossos, has thus become a real possibility.[29]

The accordance between the archaeological evidence and the Homeric image of an Achaean Minos should lead us to treat with more respect Homer's chronological indications. The Minos of Homer ruled two generations before the Trojan War (*Iliad* 13.445–54). According to Sir Arthur Evans, the palace at Knossos was destroyed in the last decade of the fifteenth century, around two centuries before the most commonly accepted date for the fall of Troy given in the literary tradition and supported in general terms by the archaeological evidence. Evans described the post-destruction period at Knossos as a degenerate phase of "squatter" occupation.[30]

This contrasts strongly with the Homeric description of Crete at the time of the Trojan War. In the Catalogue of Ships, Minos' grandson Idomeneus, ruler of Knossos and lord over many people in wide Crete, leads an expeditionary force of 80 ships (*Iliad* 2.645–52). Agamemnon himself is pictured as leading only 100 ships (*Il.* 2.576), while Menelaus has marshalled 60 (*Il.* 2.586–87). No one would put any confidence in even the relative value of these numbers, but the general Homeric picture of the strength of Knossos is suggestive, particularly if we accept the idea that the Achaean Catalogue of Ships in the *Iliad* is substantially an inheritance from the later Mycenaean period, orally transmitted through the Dark Ages.[31]

Furthermore, we are no longer faced with a clear conflict between the Homeric and the archaeological description of Knossos in the last period of the Bronze Age. At present, the date of the destruction of the palace at Knossos is the center of a lively controversy. For Leonard Palmer and J. W. Graham, the palace at Knossos was destroyed after the end of Troy VIIA, the Troy of Homer (about 1240 B.C.), and roughly at the same time as the

Mycenaean palace at Pylos. In their views, in the thirteenth century Knossos was the administrative center of a powerful dynasty of Greek kings.[32]

However this controversy may be resolved, it is clear that there is no necessity to invoke volcanic eruptions and tidal waves to explain the collapse of the Minoans. Their civilization continued, and what happened in the early fifteenth century B.C. was a transformation in the political structure of Crete, the occupation of Knossos by Greeks. As throughout history, the human element, not natural forces, was the destroyer of political structures. The Greeks occupied Knossos because they possessed a military force superior to that of the Cretans, not because a nonexistent Minoan fleet had been destroyed by a tidal wave. The Greeks continued to occupy Knossos until a superior military force broke their military power. If we possessed even a framework of Minoan political history, we could perhaps point to specific historical causes for the Hellenic military success and later collapse. As it is, we are faced simply with the fact. However, to invoke natural calamities as a cause is no more helpful and little more scientific than a Hellenistic historian's appeal to Fortuna.

Furthermore, the clear presence of Greeks at Knossos demands that we deal seriously with the possibility that the tradition of a Minoan thalassocracy may reflect the political situation of a Greek dynasty at Knossos in the fourteenth and thirteenth centuries. In terms of the archaeological material, this was the great period of cultural unity on the mainland, marked by a common tradition of pottery styles from the southwestern tip of the Peloponnese to the northwestern part of Thessaly. Most of the Mycenaean pottery found abroad is from this period, and it provides impressive evidence of widespread commercial contacts. Nearly thirty sites in Asia Minor have yielded Mycenaean pottery, and along the coast of Syria Mycenaean sherds have been found from Tell Atschana in the north to Gerar at the edge of the Sinai Peninsula.

Mycenaean contacts with Egypt were particularly intensive in the reign of Ikhnaton (1377–1358 B.C.). In the eastern Mediterranean, Mycenaean settlements have been recognized at Miletos, Phylakopi, Staphylos, Ialysos, Kos, Rhodes, and in Ugarit, Cyprus, and Egypt. In the other direction, the evidence of pottery points to fairly extensive contacts between the Mycenaean world and southern Italy, where a Rhodian trading settlement is thought to have existed at Scoglio del Tonno near Tarentum. In Sicily, Mycenaean ceramics are particularly abundant in the area around Syracuse. At the time of Xerxes' invasion, the priestess at Delphi could refer to a well-known story that Minos had died in Sicily, where he had gone in pursuit of Daedalus (Herodotus 7.70). If the story is a remembrance of actual Bronze Age contacts between Sicily and the Minoan-Mycenaean world, it must be taken to indicate that the historical Minos was an Achaean, for, as was pointed out earlier, not a single Minoan sherd has been found in Sicily.

It has been common to speak of this period as the age of "Mycenaean hegemony," a term which can be justified by neither the literary nor the archaeological evidence. It is extremely doubtful that Mycenae exercised any sort of commercial dominance in the Greek world of this period. The Late Helladic III A-B pottery (about 1400–1200 B.C.), which forms our main evidence for commercial contacts, was manufactured at a number of sites outside the Argolid. In particular, objection must be raised against the assumption that the overwhelming predominance of Mycenaean over Minoan pottery in the eastern Mediterranean after 1500 B.C. indicates that "in the fifteenth century Mycenae managed to capture [from Crete] most of the trade with Egypt, Cyprus, and the Levant in general."[33] In the first place, as argued above, the mere presence of Minoan or Mycenaean artifacts tells us nothing of whether the individual merchants transporting these objects were Greek, Cretan, or natives of Ugarit or elsewhere.

Secondly, there is no justification for the assumption that the rulers of Knossos or Mycenae sought to foster trade. In speaking of Bronze Age trade we must speak in terms of individual merchants, not of governments seeking to establish commercial empires. It remains to be established that any ancient government, whether in New Kingdom Egypt, Ugarit, Knossos, or seventh-century Corinth, was imperialistic out of a desire to corner markets and to increase exports. Whether such economic motives explain modern imperialism is doubtful, and these certainly remain to be proven for the Aegean world in the second millennium B.C. In such circumstances, it is misleading and anachronistic, to say the least, to speak of Minoan and Mycenaean commercial empires or to imply that trade rivalries played a role in the Greek conquest of Knossos or in the final destruction of Knossos. It is salutary to ponder that we possess no evidence that commercial rivalry was instrumental in provoking war and conquest in the classical Greek world.

Thus, as in the case of a Minoan Cretan commercial thalassocracy, a sea empire of Minos, the Achaean lord of Knossos two generations before the Trojan War, finds no confirmation in archaeological evidence derived from the finds of contemporary Mycenaean pottery throughout the eastern Mediterranean. In fact, this archaeological material does not indicate that any naval power dominated the Aegean world in this period, and there is no justification for the assertion that "The navy that dominated the East Mediterranean in the late Bronze Age was surely that of the Mycenaean confederation."[34] Widespread commercial contacts do not depend upon military control of the sea lanes. The Archaic Age was the great period of the expansion of Greek commerce and of colonization, and yet no state ruled the waves and never was piracy more rife.

Thus, viewed critically and historically, archaeology fails us in our search to discover a thalassocracy, whether Minoan or Achaean, in Bronze Age Greece. It remains to be asked whether there is any historical kernel in the literary tradition of Minos the thalassocrat. It must be admitted that the literary stemma for Minos the sea lord is unimpressive. Homer, who represents our best source for the image of Minos in folk memory, makes no reference to Minos as master of a maritime empire. In the *Odyssey,* Minos appears in the underworld, holding a golden rod and passing sentence on the dead. He is remembered for his kingship over Knossos and for his special relationship with Zeus, as son and as a bosom friend who every nine years held converse with the god (*Odyssey* 11.568–71; 19.178–80). A more unpleasant side to his nature may be implied in the Homeric epithet *oloophron* (*Odyssey* 11.322: "destructive-minded," "baleful"). This same portrait of Minos, divinely invested king over many in Crete, also appears in Hesiod.[35]

Among the extant sources, it is first in Herodotus that we find an explicit tradition of Minos the thalassocrat. Although Minos' descent from Zeus led Herodotus to set him apart from Polycrates, his thalassocracy was a historical possibility for Herodotus, who elsewhere refers to the Knossian's territorial conquests and his employment of Carian sailors (1.171; 3.122). Thucydides went beyond this and saw Minos' thalassocracy as the first step in the political civilization of Greece (1.4–8). Minos ruled through his navy and the colonies which he established throughout the islands. He drove piracy from the seas, thus permitting interstate commerce and navigation. The inhabitants of the seacoast now began to acquire more property and to become more settled. Their more sedentary life was due to a desire for gain. Actuated by this, the weaker citizens were willing to submit to dependence on the stronger; the more powerful men, with enlarged resources, were able to subjugate lesser cities. It is noteworthy that this most perceptive student of Greek history did not attribute mercantile motives to Minos. The Knossian cleared the sea of pirates in order to receive his tributes more safely, not in order to corner markets and to force Minoan exports upon the conquered (1.4).

Thus the literary tradition for Minos the thalassocrat can be traced back no further than the mid-fifth century B.C. What sources Herodotus drew upon cannot be determined. He refers (7.170) to Delphi's use, at the time of Xerxes' invasion, of a Cretan tradition that Minos' violent death in Sicily provoked a large-scale Cretan punitive expedition. There is no suggestion that Minos ruled a maritime empire. His purpose in going to Sicily was the punishment of Daedalus, not conquest. A single transmarine expedition does not make a thalassocracy any more than the tale of Theseus' seaborne expedition against Knossos represents a tradition of an Athenian thalassocracy in the Heroic Age.

The story of Theseus and the Minotaur has also been alleged to preserve firm recollections of Minoan Crete, above all in the word labyrinth, which is thought to have been the actual name of the Bronze Age palace at Knossos, the "Place of the Double Axe," mentioned in the Linear B tablets. This seems doubtful. The frequent assertion that the tablets at Knossos give the name "labyrinth" to the palace rests upon the assumption that the place name da-pu$_2$-ri-to, which appears clearly in only one tablet, can be identified with *labyrinthos*. To assert this identification "involves the highly uncertain assumption that the initial consonant has some intermediate sound peculiar to 'Aegean.' "[36]

The point has already been made that the palace at Knossos could be described as the "Place of the Double Axe." However, it is by no means certain that *labyrinthos* means Place of the Double Axe. No ancient writer gives this meaning. It is a modern conjecture based upon Plutarch's statement that the Lydian word for axe was *labyrs*.[37] An equally plausible derivation of *labyrinthos* is from *laura*, and its original sense would have been "a collection of narrow passages."[38]

Finally, we cannot even uncritically assume that the poor Minotaur represents a degenerate relic of the spirited bull games. As with the sphinx, which was well known in Minoan art, Egypt represents the most likely origin for the image of a human with a bull's head. It is quite possible that Theseus' slaying of the Minotaur no more reflects the realities of Minoan society than does Oedipus' destruction of the sphinx.[39] In neither case can we determine how the myth arose, and only the most uncritical Euhemerism can persuade us that either story reflects historical fact.

Thus neither archaeology nor the literary tradition permits us to assert that the tradition of Minos the thalassocrat is an actual reflection of the political history of Bronze Age Greece. It may be a literary invention. If so, its fabricators were Dorian; their motive was to provide a heroic prototype for Dorian expansion in Sicily; and their inspiration was the widespread occurrence of Minoa as a place name in the Aegean.

Modern preoccupation with Minos the pre-Hellenic Cretan has led us to forget how revered a figure Minos was in the Dorian pantheon of heroes. According to one of the genealogies of Minos, his adopted father was Asterios, the son of the daughter of Kres by Tectamus, the son of Dorus, eponymous founder of the Dorian race. According to a tradition known to Aristotle (*Politics* 2.7.2), Minos established the Cretan constitution which served as the inspiration for Lycurgus' reform of the laws of Sparta. His death occurred at the hands of the treacherous Cocalus, king of the Sicani, in what would later be the territory of Agrigentum.[40] The avenging of his death provided a noble myth to justify relentless expansion and ruthless suppression of the native Sicels and Sicanians by the Dorian colonists of Syracuse, Gela, and Agrigentum.

The origin and historical reliability of the tradition of Minos the thalassocrat is uncertain. What is certain is the fact that the literary tradition of Minos, ruler of the sea, cannot be used to support the assertion that Evans' Minoan Crete, pre-Hellenic Crete of the mid-second millennium B.C., was the site of a maritime empire exercising dominion over the Greek mainland and the islands. Evans' Minoan thalassocracy is a myth based upon an arbitrary twisting of the literary evidence and a one-sided and uncritical evaluation of the archaeological material. That it was propounded by the discoverer of Minoan civilization is understandable. It is a problem for students of historiography to determine why such a dubious theory won such wide acceptance and continues to play a major role in historical reconstructions of the Aegean world in the Bronze Age.

For us it is enough to point out how ill-founded are any attempts to establish a case for the historical existence of Atlantis upon the ephemeral foundations of a pre–Hellenic Cretan empire. Neither archaeology nor Greek mythology offers any support for the view that the tale of Atlantis reflects the imperial power and sudden disappearance of Minoan Crete. When this is combined with the clear evidence that Plato's tale of Atlantis is his own invention and not the reflection of a valid historical tradition, it becomes clear how futile must be any search for historical elements in the myth of Atlantis. Atlantis is not a remembrance of things past, but rather completely a poetic fancy. It should not be permitted to intrude into any historical reconstruction of the preclassical Mediterranean world.

It is disturbing that, in the last quarter of the twentieth century, serious scholarship is still called upon to debate the possibility that Plato's Atlantis is a remembrance of Minoan Crete. Even at a superficial glance, the equation of Atlantis with Minoan Crete is revealed as a tissuework of fabrications, a flimsy house of cards, constructed by piling dubious hypothesis upon pure speculation, cementing them together with false and misleading statements and with specious reasoning. Plato's portrait of an island-based empire, we are told, "is a startlingly accurate sketch of the Minoan empire in the sixteenth century B.C." (*The End of Atlantis*, p. 178). A dubious hypothetical empire, securely attested by neither the archaeological nor the literary sources, thus becomes the foundation for an elaborate series of arguments equating Atlantis with pre-Hellenic Crete.

The most articulate champion of the equation has summarized his case by a literary device, asking his readers to imagine that Plato is in the dock and that the case to be decided is the Atlantis story—fact or fiction (*The End of Atlantis*, pp. 176–95). Unfortunately, his argument is not very good; he seeks to overwhelm the jury with an avalanche of rhetorical half-truths and falsehoods.

"Solon's account, and possibly also a Solonian manuscript, descended to Plato by the route he indicates within his own family" (*The End of Atlantis*, p. 180). The view is at best highly debatable. Why, if the story were current, was it not known to Thucydides? Plato's contemporaries seem not to have accepted the possibility that the story represented authentic history, and succeeding generations of Athenian rhetoricians, always eager for an attempt to glorify the city, ignore Atlantis entirely, thus suggesting that they viewed it as a completely fictional utopia.

"But surely the picture of an island-centred empire dominating other islands and parts of a continent is a very unlikely fiction for a romancer to have devised, . . ." (*The End of Atlantis*, p. 178). Plato, however, knew intimately just such an island-centered empire, the realm of Dionysius of Syracuse, which dominated Sicily, other islands, and such parts of the opposing continent as southern Italy, Ancona, and Molossia.

" 'There were bulls . . . and the ten kings, being left alone in the temple [of Poseidon], . . . hunted the bulls, without weapons, but with staves and nooses' (*Critias*, 119d–e). A feature of the bull-ring at Knossos, which distinguishes it from all other bull 'fights' . . . was that the toreadors were completely unarmed" (*The End of Atlantis*, p. 182). But there is another, more plausible equation to be made. Plato takes great care to place his tale of Atlantis within an Egyptian context, and the obvious parallel is the Egyptian royal ceremony of the unarmed pharaoh lassoing the bull, a frequent scene in Egyptian art of all periods. Egypt is the ultimate source for the imagery on the Vapheio cups, which are often cited as Minoan parallels for Plato's picture. The bull games at Knossos should not even enter the discussion since, so far as anyone knows, the bulls were not lassoed as part of the performance.

"The site of the primeval 'earthborn' dwellers in Atlantis was on a low hill about 50 *stadia* inland, near a very fertile plain and halfway along the coast of the island (*Critias*, 113c). The hill was five *stadia* in diameter (*Critias*, 116a). . . . The figures are . . . very appropriate to the actual site of Knossos, . . ." (*The End of Atlantis*, p. 181). This kind of speculation only serves to confuse the issue.

Plato's figures are no more appropriate to Knossos than they are to Agrigentum in Sicily, or other sites that might be named. In the same way, it is hardly to the point to note that Plato's description of the rest of the island of Atlantis recalls the southern coast of Crete. It equally recalls Sicily. Once again, it was Sicily, not Crete, which Plato knew and toward which his Athenian contemporaries, who awarded Dionysius a drama award, were drawn.

"Here the Atlanteans built their palace '... which they continued to ornament in successive generations, ... until they made the building a marvel to behold for size and beauty.' (*Critias,* 115 c–d) During ... six centuries [i.e., 2000–1400 B.C.] the palace [at Knossos] was frequently rebuilt and enlarged until it covered an area of about 20,000 sq. m. It was, and to some extent still is, 'a marvel to behold for size and beauty'" (*The End of Atlantis,* p. 181). But there are other, better comparisons to be made. In their descriptions of eastern cities such as Babylon and Ecbatana, both Herodotus and Ctesias speak of the circles of walls, canals, elaborate palaces surrounded by circular walls, and temples covered with gold and filled with statues, which are the central features of Plato's Atlantis and which are entirely lacking at Knossos. Herodotus' Ecbatana had seven circles of walls, whose turrets were black, white, red, blue, vermilion, silver, and gold. Plato uses the colors black, white, and red for the stones of his building and four metals of increasing value, with silver and gold at the end to cover his wall rings. It would appear, then, that Plato's Atlantis is his own poetic invention, but that in the details of his description he was clearly influenced by the contemporary situation in Sicily and by contemporary Greek knowledge of Near Eastern urban and palace complexes.[41]

It is hoped that throughout this farce of a trial Plato has remained silent. His Atlantis needs no defense. The realization that Plato has nothing to do with contemporary Atlantean mania is the sole consolation to be drawn from a refutation of the equation of Minoan Crete with Atlantis. In order to make the equation, archaeologists and philologists have transformed every major feature of his story. Plato places Atlantis in the Atlantic. His modern "defenders" remove it to the Mediterranean. From a no longer extant island, it miraculously reappears as Crete. Plato securely places his story 9,000 years before his time. His advocates tell us that he meant 900. He measures the plain around Atlantis at 3,000 by

2,000 stadia; what he meant was 300 by 200. And so on, until, by a process of bowdlerization, Plato's Atlantis is transmuted into a salable product, which can exploit public interest in archaeology, ignorant fantasies about Bermuda Triangles and Shangri-Las, and contemporary morbid fascination with disasters. Commercialism has thus transformed an instructive philosophical utopia into a harbinger of *The Towering Inferno* and *Krakatoa, East of Java.* It is no tribute that classical scholarship has condoned and abetted this travesty.

THE GEOLOGICAL PERSPECTIVE

I. Atlantis from the Geologic Point of View

DOROTHY B. VITALIANO

Inasmuch as all references to Atlantis stem from Plato and no other source, in deciding whether it is fact or fiction—or, to put it another way, whether it is legend or myth—we are faced with three options: we can take everything Plato says quite literally; we can take his words seriously but not literally; or we can take Atlantis as purely and simply his invention. This essay examines each of these alternatives from the point of view of its geologic validity.

But first it would be well to make clear exactly what is intended here by the terms "myth" and "legend," for even experts on such matters do not agree among themselves on their definition. In analyzing the folklore of geology[1] it is most convenient to consider myths to be those traditions which are imaginative attempts to explain the natural world, and legends those which have at their core real persons or events. The latter would be called myths in the old sense of Euhemerus, the Sicilian philosopher who believed the gods of mythology were real personages who became deified in the course of time. In our view, myths by definition are purely imaginary, and therefore any tale which is euhemeristic is not a myth but a legend.

In practice it is often quite impossible to know whether there is a grain of fact in a given tale. The supposedly universal flood tradition is very frequently cited in support of the reality of Atlantis. But Sir James Frazer[2] analyzed flood traditions from all parts of the world and concluded that some were imaginative attempts to explain observed natural features (myths, in our definition), while others, including the biblical Flood, were memories of real disasters (legends, in our definition). How very easily a legend can come into being as a result of a natural disaster is exemplified by the Tarawera eruption of 1886 in New Zealand, which overwhelmed the village of Te Ariki and its inhabitants. Not long after, there arose a legend, complete with the supernatural, which blamed the eruption on a demon named Tamaohoi, long imprisoned in the mountain and summoned forth by one of his descendants, a tohunga (medicine man or priest) named Tuhoto, to punish the villagers for their decline in morals. The tohunga of the village at the time of the eruption was named Tuhoto, and he did have an ancestor named Tamaohoi.

The current popular concept of Atlantis was crystallized by Ignatius Donnelly in a book entitled *Atlantis: The Antediluvian World,* published in 1882.[3] Since that book is still being sold in bookstores everywhere and has provided the basis for numerous other works, it is desirable to explain why his literal interpretation of Plato's description is utterly inconsistent with modern scientific knowledge. Donnelly outlined thirteen propositions, in support of which he then proceeded to marshal all kinds of evidence. Only two of these propositions are relevant to a geologically oriented discussion:

Proposition #1. "That there once existed in the Atlantic Ocean, opposite the mouth of the Mediterranean Sea, a large island, which was the remnant of an Atlantic continent, and known to the ancient world as Atlantis."

Proposition #12. "That Atlantis perished in a terrible convulsion of nature, in which the whole island sunk into the ocean, with nearly all its inhabitants."

Let us consider the latter proposition first. In support, Donnelly pointed out that vast landmasses have risen and sunk throughout geologic history, and that sizable areas have become permanently submerged as a result of seismic or volcanic activity. Both these statements are true individually, but they refer to processes which occur on vastly different scales, and they do not add up to mean that a large island can be submerged in as little as a day and a night, the time allotted by Plato to the catastrophe which overwhelmed Atlantis. Continent-sized landmasses have indeed risen and sunk in the course of geologic time; that is an exceedingly slow process which has gone on constantly and is going on even now in various parts of the world. On the other hand, suddenly and catastrophically submerged areas, usually coastal areas depressed as a result of an earthquake, or in rare cases a collapsing volcanic island such as Krakatoa in 1883 or Santorini in the fifteenth century B.C.,[4] are seldom larger than a few dozen square miles.

To support his proposition #1, that Atlantis was the remnant of a continent that once existed in the Atlantic Ocean, Donnelly pointed to the discovery, recent in his time, of a ridge in the middle of the North Atlantic, which he and many others took to be a landmass which had sunk, leaving only its highest peaks above water to form the Azores and other mid-Atlantic islands. He also cited certain similarities in the flora and fauna of the Old and New Worlds which suggested a land connection in the recent (post-glacial) past.

In the light of what is known today about the ocean floors we can definitely rule out the possibility of a sunken landmass of any substantial size in the Atlantic, or, for that matter, in any other ocean basin. It has now been established—from the speed at which earthquake vibrations propagate through the earth—that the material of the earth's crust[5] underlying the continents (including their submerged margins) is different from the material underlying the ocean floors; nowhere in the ocean basins is there any sign of a large mass of continental-type crust which could represent a submerged continent.

The past twenty-five years have seen a tremendous revolution in geologic thought. It is now apparent that the ocean basins are not permanent features of the globe, as was once believed. Beginning from its southern end, the Atlantic Ocean began to open up more than a hundred million years ago, at the end of the Cretaceous period, and its floor is still spreading. Far from being a foundered landmass, the Mid-Atlantic Ridge is part of a global feature which is one of the youngest large-scale features on the face of the earth. It is being built up on the ocean floor of new material erupted from deep in the earth's mantle along a vast rift along its center. As new material fills the rift, the opposite sides, moving as huge "plates" of lithosphere sliding on a weaker, somewhat plastic layer in the mantle, drift slowly apart, carrying the continents apart with them.[6]

This new version of the old continental drift theory does away with the need for the "land bridges" across the Atlantic once postulated by geologists, but in any case those Atlantic land bridges were believed to have existed only up to the end of the Cretaceous period; after that, the flora and fauna on the opposite sides of the ocean developed independently.

The similarities in flora and fauna cited by Donnelly date from a much later time—for instance, the finding of the hairy mammoth, woolly rhinoceros, Irish elk, muskox, reindeer, and the like in "postglacial" deposits in both Europe and North America. However, what was considered to be "postglacial" in Donnelly's time included much that is now considered to be Pleistocene; the end of the Ice Age is now put at 10,000–11,000 years ago, on the basis of radiocarbon dating. Before that, animals and eventually man had several opportunities, beginning as long as eight million years ago, to migrate between Eurasia and North America across what is now Bering Strait;[7] for it was dry land at the times when glaciation was at a maximum and, with so much of the earth's water locked up in the form of ice, sea level was correspondingly lower. Some of the animals, like the mammoth, died out in both the Old and New Worlds, while others survived in one or the other, or both. There is no need to invoke an Atlantic landmass to explain their presence in Pleistocene deposits on both sides of the ocean. Nor is an intervening landmass necessary to explain similarities in plant species—not when seeds or sprouts could so easily have been carried by driftwood or migrating birds at any time.

The second alternative, that Plato should be taken seriously but not literally, offers a very wide choice of times and places. But which parts of his description should be accepted as correct, and which as distorted or incorrect?

Obviously, it does not help to change only the time element while leaving the site in the Atlantic, as did the late Scottish mythologist Lewis Spence, for instance. While generally accepting Donnelly's premises, he recognized the inconsistency between the Bronze Age civilization described by Plato and the dating of its destruction as 9,000 years before Solon's time, or about 11,500 years ago. He suggested[8] that the destruction of Atlantis was the last event in the breakup of a large continent which formerly occupied much of the North Atlantic. Two large remnants, "Antillia" and Atlantis, lasted until 25,000 years ago; some of Antillia survives as the present West Indies, but Atlantis was completely destroyed in about 10,000 B.C. The superior race which inhabited Atlantis was the Palaeolithic Crô-Magnon people, some of whom survived the destruction and made their way to Europe.

As part of his geologic evidence, Spence cited what is still a favorite argument of proponents of an Atlantic site,[9] even though it is based on an erroneous interpretation of a geologic observation. In fishing for a broken cable about 500 miles north of the Azores in 1898, the grappling hook brought up splinters of rock obviously chipped from a bedrock outcrop at a depth of 1,700 fathoms (more than 10,000 feet). These chips were of tachylite, a basaltic glass. These rocks excited the interest of a French geologist[10] who recalled observations that had been made on the lavas of Mont Pelée in Martinique. There, lavas which had congealed in the open air were vitreous, whereas lavas which had cooled under a cover of previously solidified rocks formed ordinary finely crystalline basalt. Assuming, quite incorrectly, that it was pressure that made the difference, he concluded that the tachylite from the ocean floor must have formed at the earth's surface, under atmospheric pressure, and from that he inferred that this part of the ocean floor had sunk by nearly two miles. In fact, however, it is not pressure which determines whether lava will crystallize or form glass, but the rate of cooling. A lava which is quenched rapidly, either upon meeting cool air or upon coming into contact with cold water, will not have time to crystallize and will form a glassy rock. Basaltic glass is known to have been formed at depths of 17,000 feet or more,[11] so there is no reason why the rock brought up by the grappling iron could not have been produced right where it was found.

With an Atlantic site ruled out as physically impossible, all arguments based on racial, linguistic, or other cultural similarities on both sides of the ocean (which would include the rest of Donnelly's 13 propositions) must collapse. Either they are not real similarities at all (and some of them have already been disproved),[12] or they must be explained in other ways, including mere coincidence.

However, our second alternative still offers a very wide choice of locations outside of the Atlantic Ocean, particularly if the time element is considered to be distorted as well as the location. The following alternative sites have been proposed, according to L. Sprague de Camp's *Lost Continents*:[13] North Africa, Ceylon, North America, Crete, Mongolia, Spitsbergen, Carthage, Gades (ancient Cadiz), the Atlas Mountains, Tartessos (in Spain), South Africa, Tunisia, Malta, the Mediterranean Sea off the coast of Tunisia, Spain, central France, the Caucasus, the western Mediterranean, the North Sea, the Sahara Desert, East Prussia and the Baltic Sea, the Ahaggar Mountains (Algeria), Greenland, Iran, Mexico, Central America, Iraq, Crimea, the West Indies, Belgium and the Netherlands, Sweden, Catalonia, the British Isles, the Arctic, a North Polar continent, a Pacific continent, a South Pacific continent including South America and Australia, and the Indian Ocean. To de Camp's list there can be added the Aegean Sea near Crete[14] and, more recently, Bimini[15] and the Greek island of Santorini (Thera) plus Crete.[16]

By accepting as true those details of Plato's description of Atlantis which seem to fit one of these presumed sites and taking as distortions those which do not fit, some sort of case can be made for any of them except the ocean basins, which are open to the same objection as the Atlantic site—there are no remnants of continental crust which could represent a large foundered landmass. (Thus even if one invokes some extraterrestrial agency to explain how a large island could be destroyed in a single cataclysm, it does not help; its remnants would be recognizable.)

One of those sites is worth a closer look. Not only is it enjoying much publicity at present, but it also is the only one that offers both of what might be considered the essential elements of the Atlantis story—a superior civilization and a disappearing island.

As long ago as 1909 an anonymous letter to the London *Times* pointed out some rather striking resemblances between Minoan Crete and Atlantis. The Minoan civilization, at that time only recently discovered, flourished from about 3000 B.C. to about 1450 B.C. During that time the Minoans became the dominant political and economic force in the Aegean area and enjoyed a standard of living unequalled anywhere for a long time after their downfall. Their prosperity was based on sea trade with lands as far away as Egypt, the Near East, and the shores of the Tyrrhenian Sea, as well as with their more immediate neighbors in the Aegean. Then, apparently while they were still at the peak of their power, the civilization of the Minoans collapsed with astonishing abruptness. The Minoan people themselves were not driven out and supplanted by aliens, but their rulers were; as it turned out, the new rulers were Mycenaeans from the Greek mainland. At the time of the take-over—virtually simultaneous with it, so far as can be read from the archaeological record—there was wholesale destruction on Crete and other Minoan island dependencies. Not only were all but one of the Minoan palaces (Knossos) and all of the mansions razed, but sometimes whole cities too. None of the ruined palaces was ever rebuilt, as they always had been after severe earthquakes, and in some cases entire cities or towns were abandoned forever.

The anonymous letter-writer to the *Times,* who later revealed himself to be the classical scholar K. T. Frost, amplified his suggestion in an article published in 1913.[17] From the Egyptian point of view, he reasoned, the sudden breaking off of the visits of traders from Crete might easily have suggested that the Minoans had sunk into the sea.

Frost's suggestion received no more attention than many another until the 1960s, when A. G. Galanopoulos, a Greek seismologist, began publishing a series of papers and finally a book[18] linking Atlantis not only to Crete and the Minoans, but also to Santorini[19] and its Bronze Age eruption. That eruption culminated in the collapse of the center of the island and totally destroyed a very prosperous settlement on the island. Like Frost, Galanopoulos believes in the reality of the Egyptian document brought back to Greece by Solon and tries to reconcile the inconsistencies between the geographic facts and Plato's description by postulating a translation error which caused all dimensions given in hundreds of units to come out as thousands and thus demanded that Plato remove Atlantis to the Atlantic Ocean, since the Mediterranean could not accommodate so large a land. Galanopoulos further assumes that Plato was speaking of two different parts of Atlantis, the Metropolis of Atlantis, which was the island of Santorini itself, and the plain around the Royal City, which was the Mesara plain in southern Crete.

The translation error argument is a brilliant one, but Galanopoulos seriously weakens his case by insisting on a too-literal interpretation of Plato's description. For instance, in the present configuration of the bottom of the bay which now occupies the center of Santorini (figure 3), he sees traces of the Metropolis of Atlantis, complete with its concentric harbors. However, that topography

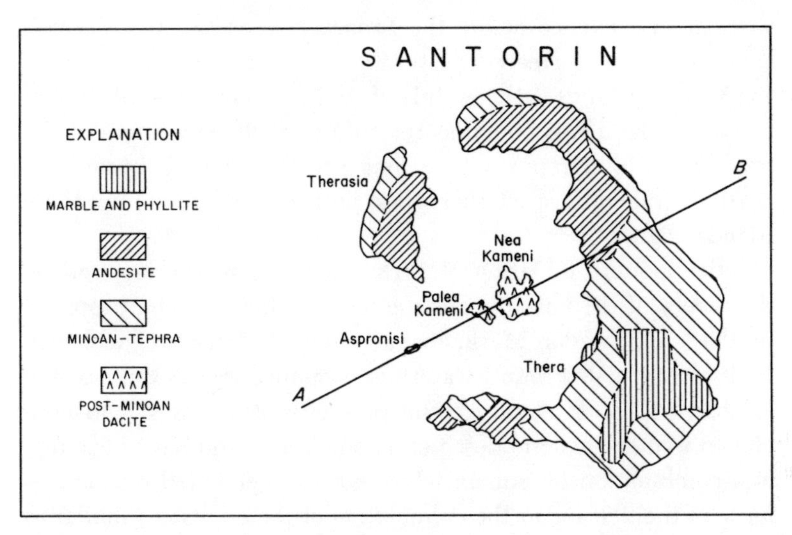

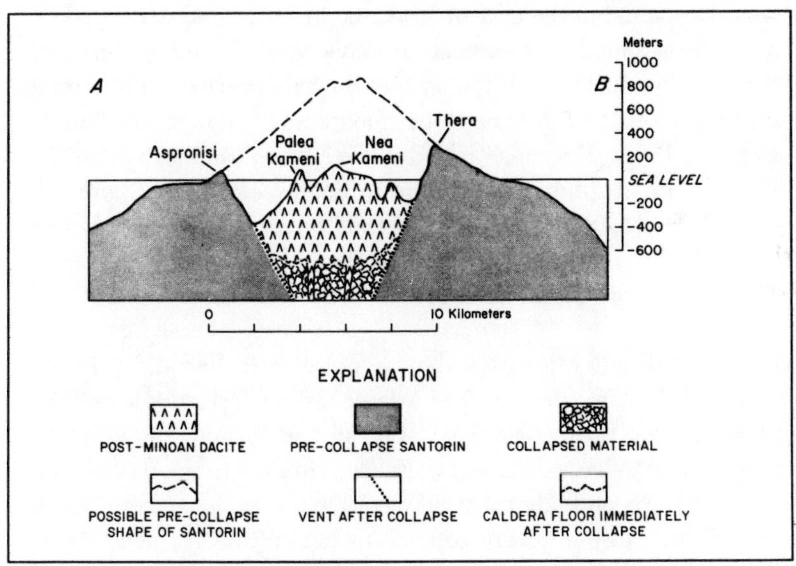

Figure 3. Santorini: geologic configuration, from D. B. Vitaliano, *Legends of the Earth,* by permission of Indiana University Press.

was not in existence before the Bronze Age eruption of the volcano; it has been created by subsequent activity which built up the Kameni Islands in the middle of the bay, to which a substantial amount of land was added as recently as 1926. Any traces of the precollapse topography would long since have been buried beneath the pile of lava whose highest portions emerge to form these islands (figure 3).[20]

Galanopoulos' updating of Frost's suggestion was inspired by the theory of the volcanic destruction of Minoan Crete, proposed by the late Spyridon Marinatos, an eminent Greek archaeologist. In 1939 Marinatos found waterborne pumice in the ruins of the Minoan palace at Amnisos, the port city of Knossos, and concluded that the general destruction on Crete could have been due to a combination of tsunamis (sea waves) generated by the collapse of the volcano at the culmination of the eruption (similar to what happened in the case of Krakatoa in 1883) and earthquakes, which he assumed—not quite accurately—would have accompanied the eruption. In 1965 this theory found what appeared to be strong support when two American oceanographers, Dragoslav Ninkovich and Bruce Heezen,[21] found a layer of volcanic ash from the Bronze Age eruption of Santorini in deep-sea sediment cores all around the eastern end of Crete, thus proving that a blanket of ash must have covered at least that part of the island (figure 4). This could more plausibly account for the abandonment of inland sites on Crete.

The validity of Marinatos' theory, and with it the validity of the idea that the Minoans were the Atlanteans in a historical sense, depends on several factors. First and most important, the eruption would have to have occurred quite close in time to the destruction on Crete. Second, the ashfall would have to have been thick enough to cause a severe setback to agriculture for some time. Third, the collapse of the volcano would have to have occurred at the climax of the eruption and suddenly enough to produce major tsunamis capable of doing extensive damage to Cretan ports and shipping, and fourth, there would have to have been an earth-

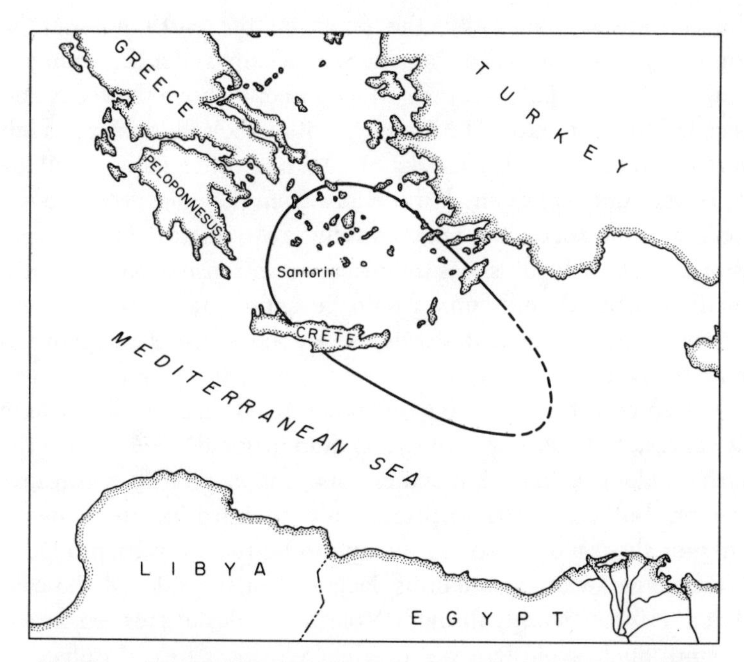

Figure 4. Distribution of tephra from the Bronze Age eruption of Santorini, from D. B. Vitaliano, *Legends of the Earth,* by permission of Indiana University Press.

quake, or a series of earthquakes, strong enough to topple buildings and even whole cities over a very wide area on Crete, but at the same time selective enough to cause only minor damage at Knossos.

Let us consider these factors in reverse order: earthquakes, tsunamis, ashfall, and timing.

Earthquakes. There are two kinds of earthquakes: tectonic and volcanic. The vast majority are tectonic. They are caused by sudden disturbances, usually rupturing in the solid rock, in the earth's crust or upper mantle, and are classified as shallow, intermediate, or deep (0–70, 70–300, and over 300 kilometers, respectively), depending on the depth at which the disturbance occurs. The amount of energy released when this occurs determines the *magnitude* of the earthquake. Naturally, the point on the earth nearest the source, or *focus*, of the earthquake will usually suffer the strongest shaking; it is the point on the surface directly above the focus and is called the *epicenter*. The *intensity* with which the shaking is felt at the surface, which is what determines how much damage will be done, dies out rapidly in all directions from the epicenter, and the shallower the focus, the more rapidly it attenuates. Thus a very strong shallow-focus shock might cause extensive damage in a small area but do only minor damage not too far away, whereas a very strong intermediate-focus shock could cause damage over a very wide area.

Volcanic earthquakes, on the other hand, are produced as a direct result of volcanic activity. As fluid magma[22] rises toward the surface along a line of weakness, its motion sets up a constant tremor, but that is perceptible only to sensitive instruments. Sharper shocks, often strong enough to be felt, may be produced if the magma causes actual displacement of the sides of the conduit as it forces its way through. Volcanic explosions also shake the ground. Such explosions occur when volatile gases, dissolved in the magma under great pressure at depth, are suddenly liberated when the pressure is released as it nears the surface. Repeated explosions of this kind, of varying degrees of intensity, are the rule in most eruptions, and in fact eruptions are classified according to the degree of explosivity, which in turn depends to a great extent on the chemical composition of the magma. (The Santorini eruption in the Bronze Age was of the most highly explosive type, a pumice eruption of dacitic magma.) Extremely violent explosions, and with them sharper shocks, can also be produced if water penetrating through fissures comes in contact with hot rising magma.

Volcanic earthquakes are very shallow compared to tectonic earthquakes, and usually very weak; thus they are felt only in the vicinity of an erupting (or about-to-erupt) volcano and seldom are strong enough to do damage even there. Only a tectonic earthquake could have been responsible for structural damage as far away as Crete, and if one happened to occur just while Santorini was in eruption it would have been very much of a coincidence. However, there is no real reason why one or more tectonic earthquakes could not have occurred within months or a few years of the eruption, and from our vantage point they might appear to have been simultaneous. But then it still remains to be explained how Knossos alone was spared when buildings in all other parts of eastern Crete were leveled. No single strong shock could have been that selective, whereas too many smaller local ones in too short a time are needed to cause such widespread damage. Earthquakes alone cannot explain the structural damage on Crete.

Tsunamis. Structural damage could have been inflicted on the shores of Crete, if one or more of these frightful sea waves was generated when the Santorini volcano collapsed. In the analogous case of Krakatoa, practically all of the tremendous loss of life (estimated at 36,000 dead, at least) was caused by the last and highest of the waves, generated by the collapse of the volcano at the climax of the eruption. But formidable as they are, tsunamis cannot accomplish some of the prodigious feats ascribed to them in a number of recent publications which have attempted to assess their probable impact on Crete.

Tsunamis are also called "seismic sea waves"[23] because they usually are associated with earthquakes. But they are not caused by earthquake vibrations *per se;* otherwise every submarine shock would be accompanied by one, and fortunately only a small proportion of such shocks do cause them. Occasionally, too, there are tsunamis which have nothing to do with earthquakes.

Tsunamis are caused by the sudden displacement of very large masses of water. Faulting on the sea floor is one such displacement, and an even more common kind is a submarine landslide triggered by an earthquake. Submarine volcanic activity may suddenly displace a large volume of water if a huge gas bubble is expelled explosively on the sea floor. And specifically pertinent to the matter in hand, the collapse of a volcanic island into the void left after vast amounts of material are erupted is still another kind of tsunami-generating disturbance. In an island eruption huge waves might also be created if stupendous amounts of volcanic ejecta fall onto the sea surface all at once after an especially violent explosion; this seems to have happened in the final paroxysms of Krakatoa.

How big a tsunami will be generated by a collapsing island depends on how much material is engulfed at any one time. Krakatoa went down in several huge "gulps" hours apart, each of them creating a large train of waves; but as mentioned above, only the last one was disastrous.

Once generated, a tsunami spreads out rapidly from the point of origin, losing height at a rate proportional to the square of the distance traveled. Other things being equal, it would reach equidistant shores at the same time and with the same height, but in nature "other things" are never equal. The rate of propagation of the wave depends on the water depth (the deeper the water, the faster it travels; in the open sea tsunamis can travel as fast as 500 miles per hour), and the depth is never constant. Wave interference is set up by the presence of islands in the path of travel or when the wave impinges on a coast. Thus the wave soon becomes a train of long, low swells (up to about 400 miles from crest to crest has been measured) only a very few feet high. To ships at sea such a gentle rise and fall is imperceptible. It is when the tremendous amount of water involved in such a wave piles up on a shelving shore that trouble ensues. How high it will rise on a given shore depends not only on its original height, but even more on the precise topography of the shore and sea-bottom at that particular place. On entering a funnel-shaped bay the water piles up higher and higher as the bay narrows. On the other hand, a stretch of coast protected by an offshore island might suffer relatively little. The angle of approach of the tsunami also affects the potential run-up height. In March 1957 a tsunami from an Aleutian Island earthquake struck the island of Hawaii. In the harbor of Hilo it reached a height of 35 feet and inflicted great damage, but on another part of the coast of the same island it rose only 2 feet.[24]

It is reasonable to assume that the collapse of Santorini after the Bronze Age eruption probably generated one or more tsunamis, but what their original height may have been can only be conjectured. Any calculations based on the assumption that the entire mass collapsed all at once should be rejected out of hand, however, for it is most unlikely that it happened in that fashion. At the same time, it cannot be ruled out that the opposite occurred, namely that the collapse was a very gradual one (Askja in Iceland took fifteen years to collapse after its 1875 eruption), and in that case no destructive waves would have reached Crete.

Whatever tsunamis did reach Cretan shores could not have reached the same height at all points and thus would not have been equally destructive everywhere. But where they were worst, the damage could have been vast. The loss of a port city and many of its inhabitants, together with whatever ships were in the harbor at the time, certainly would have been a serious blow to a nation dependent on sea trade for its economic health, and the loss of more than one port proportionately more serious. But would *every* port and *every* ship have been destroyed? Hardly likely. Those ships which happened to be sailing close to the shore ran the risk of being wrecked, but those in the open sea would not have been affected, and those in foreign ports which were spared the fury of the far-traveling waves, thanks to a fortunate location with respect to the approach of the tsunamis, would likewise have been out of reach of harm. Tsunamis might account for damage to life and property on some but not all parts of the coast of Crete, but not for complete annihilation of the fleet and total destruction of all the ports.

Ashfall. A heavy ashfall can cause roofs to collapse, but, more important, it can destroy vegetation and ruin land for agricultural purposes for some time. The effects of an ashfall likewise depend on several factors: the initial thickness of the fall, the chemical composition of the ash, the topography of the land covered, the climate, even the season in which it falls.

How thick a blanket of ash fell on Crete, and what might its effects have been? From the evidence of the relatively few deep-sea cores so far available, it has been estimated that an average of about 10 centimeters (4 inches) of ash fell over the eastern end of Crete.[25] The layer would not have been uniformly thick, for light pumiceous ash drifts like snow and, once fallen, it is constantly redistributed by wind and rain (and on steep slopes, often just by gravity alone) until it ultimately finds its way into the sea.

Unless they were completely demoralized by panic, the Minoans probably would have reacted in the natural way when they saw ash piling up on their roofs, which is to sweep it off before the roof can cave in. Even if they neglected this rather elementary precaution, well-constructed roofs should have withstood a few inches of light ash. Any structural damage to buildings caused by the weight of the ash should not have been irreparable, in any case.

Damage to vegetation would have been a much more serious matter, particularly in the beginning. From the pattern of distribution of the ash layer in the deep-sea cores it has been inferred that the eruption occurred in the summer when the prevailing winds are from the northwest, which is when crops would be most vulnerable. Low-growing plants such as vegetables and grain and pasturage could have been irretrievably lost, particularly as they would most likely have been grown on low, level areas where the ash would pile up to greater than average thickness. Whatever was not smothered by the ash could have been sandblasted by wind-driven particles of the ash (which consists of tiny shards of volcanic glass), or possibly burned by noxious gases carried with the ash particles (ash from the Katmai eruption in Alaska in 1912 carried sulfur dioxide which reacted with rain to form sulfuric acid,[26] and ash from eruptions in Iceland has sometimes carried fluorine as well as sulfur dioxide[27]). But in general, except for possible damage to leaves from the sandblasting effect and acids, if any, and from the breaking of branches under the weight of the ash, trees and vines should not have suffered permanent damage.

As soon as the ash ceased falling, or even while it was still coming down, the forces of erosion would have begun to redistribute it. Steep slopes would have been stripped of it first, probably to the further detriment of anything growing at the foot of the slopes, where the material slumping down or washed down would pile up even more deeply. But in modern eruptions moderate amounts of ash—up to a foot or so—have often proved to be beneficial in the long run, acting as mulch to hold moisture. In the case of Katmai, for instance, the recovery of vegetation was much more rapid than expected (three years rather than the initially estimated ten), and all the credit is given to the mulching effect; for like the Santorini ash, the Katmai ash contained no more chemical nutrients than plain quartz sand.[28] On Crete, with its drier climate, recovery would have been slower, not only because the lower rainfall would mean less water to be conserved by the mulch effect, but also because it would mean less runoff to wash away the ash. But this would be counteracted to some extent by the fact that most of Crete's precipitation is concentrated in torrential seasonal rains, whose potential erosional power is very much greater than that of the same amount of water falling gently throughout the year. The rugged topography characteristic of much of Crete would also mean accelerated erosion of any material lying loose on its surface.

Thus the net effects of the ashfall on Crete would no doubt have been seriously disruptive at first, but surely an average thickness of more than four inches would be needed to cause a very lasting setback to the Minoan agricultural economy. It is hoped that the results of a deep-sea coring expedition in the fall of 1975 will yield a more precise idea of the amount of ash that fell on Crete from the Bronze Age eruption of Santorini.

Timing of the eruption. Before we can say that Minoan Crete was destroyed as a direct result of the Bronze Age eruption of Santorini, thereby fulfilling the essential requirements for its candidacy as Atlantis, it must be established that the collapse of Minoan power followed hard on the heels of the eruption. But the exact timing is difficult to establish. The best radiocarbon dates so far have an uncertainty of ± 44 years, which is far too imprecise in this case.

Archaeologists assign absolute (calendar) dates to cultural stages on the basis of pottery and other artifacts which can be cross-correlated with other firmly dated cultures. Stratigraphic sequences have been worked out for individual Minoan sites on Crete, Santorini, and other Aegean islands where the ruins have yielded distinct sequences of pottery from superimposed levels, and some of these can be tied in with the well-established Egyptian chronology. But correlations between the individual Minoan sites are not always clear.

The currently accepted date for the general destruction on Crete and at other Minoan sites is 1450 B.C. However, the ruins buried under the very thick pile of pumice and ash on Santorini itself (at Akrotiri) have yielded no pottery which can be firmly dated as much younger than 1500 B.C., even after eight productive seasons of excavation. A 50-year gap—about two generations—is far too wide for a direct cause-and-effect relationship between the eruption and the eclipse of Minoan civilization. This gap must be closed or at least narrowed substantially if the idea of the volcanic destruction of Minoan Crete is to be accepted. Various ways of doing so have been proposed.

The earlier interpretation of the layers of pumice and ash overlying the ruins on Thera[29] accorded perfectly with Marinatos' theory. The bottom layer, of coarse lump pumice, represented a violent outbreak which obliterated the settlement and thus left nothing for the inhabitants (who apparently escaped in time, for no bodies and few valuables have been found) to return to. A second layer, consisting of fine-grained, stratified, and sometimes crossbedded ash, was thought to represent an interval during which mild intermittent activity alternated with periods of erosion and redeposition. This interval, whose duration it is impossible to estimate from the geologic evidence alone, could be taken to correspond to the last 50 years or so of Minoan supremacy, ending in 1450 B.C. Then the very thick and chaotic upper layer of ash would correspond to the final and most violent phase of the eruption, the phase which showered ash on Crete and presumably ended with the tsunami-generating collapse. Unfortunately, international experts in volcanology who visited Santorini in 1969 (on the occasion of the First International Scientific Congress on the Volcano of Thera) were strongly of the opinion that an eruption of this type could not possibly have lasted more than three or four years from start to finish and more probably was of the order of weeks or months.[30] The stratified middle layer, they pointed out, could easily be the product of a recently recognized eruptive mechanism known as "base surge," which can produce such structures in a matter of hours.[31]

Marinatos himself believed that the inhabitants on Thera were frightened away by an earthquake and never returned. There is indeed evidence of earthquake damage on Thera before the eruption.[32] However, that damage does not seem to have been extensive enough to have kept them away for as long as 50 years. Throughout Mediterranean history settlements severely damaged by earthquakes have been temporarily abandoned, but never for more than two or three years, if that long. Moreover, there is some indication that the earthquake occurred immediately before (or even accompanying) the first violent pumice-producing explosions. This evidence consists of fissures filled with nothing but pumice. Had those fissures opened up even a short time before the pumice fell, other debris would have found its way into them first.[33]

Another idea is that the eruption occurred some time around 1500 B.C., but the collapse was delayed until 1450 B.C.[34] In that case the Minoans could have survived the effects of the ashfall only to succumb to a second blow dealt by the waves, particularly if the collapse at Santorini was triggered by an earthquake. However, it is geologically implausible for the collapse to have been delayed so long after the creation of the void whence the vast quantities of ejecta had been spewed out. The very violence of the final explosions might have rendered the roof very unstable.[35] Furthermore, invoking an earthquake (still needed to account for damage inland) runs into the objection raised above, namely the impossibility of having widespread structural damage from which Knossos alone was somehow exempted.

Yet another suggestion, one which would accept the 1450 date for the eruption and at the same time explain the virtual absence on Thera of "Marine Style" pottery—the style diagnostic of the 1500–1450 B.C. (Late Minoan I B) period, which was manufactured on Crete—is that the Marine Style ware was never imported there. But that settlement was a very prosperous one, with many fine houses, and the highly prized Marine Style ware is known from the ruins of much less sophisticated communities, and from places much farther away from Crete.[36] The absence of pottery definitely characteristic of the last phase of Minoan dominance suggests that Thera was destroyed before that style could be imported, which should have been soon after it became available.

J. V. Luce is skeptical as to the significance of the Marine Style, doubting that 50 years were needed to produce all of it that is known; he believes that the abandonment of Thera and the general destruction on Crete both occurred in 1470 B.C.[37]

There is only one way to pin down the time of the eruption precisely with respect to the stages of Minoan culture, which is to find traces of the volcanic ash from that eruption in firmly dated levels in Minoan ruins, and under such conditions that the particles found can confidently be assumed to have been collected from where they became lodged when they first fell. If such particles could be found in levels which ceased to be occupied in about 1500 B.C., then the eruption must have occurred no later than that date. Conversely, if particles are always absent below the 1450 B.C. level, then the eruption might well have played a large part in the general destruction of Minoan Crete.

So far, soil samples collected from crevices in Minoan ruins have been examined from several sites on Crete, but only at one site, Kato Zakro at the eastern end of the island, was the crucial 1500 B.C. (Late Minoan I A) level sampled under conditions precluding contamination.[38] Nevertheless, it is significant that this level did contain unmistakable traces of the Bronze Age ash. If this very preliminary result is confirmed by further work at other Minoan sites,[39] it can only mean that the Bronze Age eruption at best was just one factor which contributed to the downfall of the Minoans, but could not have been the immediate cause.

Another piece of evidence that the eruption must have preceded the final destruction on Crete by a certain interval of time—though just how long an interval cannot be ascertained—is the finding of what apparently were votive offerings of pumice in the palace at Kato Zakro and the villa at Nirou Khani.[40] Obviously the pumice, which was produced in the first climactic paroxysms of the eruption and was followed very shortly by the final ash-producing bursts, had already floated ashore on Crete in order for it to have been used in the ritual (to placate the gods?), which implies that the buildings in which it was found had not been destroyed as a result of any phenomena attendant upon the finale of the eruption. Also, at Amnisos a guide showed me the spot where Marinatos had found the pumice which first caused him to look to Santorini for the explanation of the destruction. It was not scattered throughout the ruins, as would be expected if the pumice had been washed ashore into the remains of a palace destroyed by a tsunami, but was concentrated in a walled receptacle with a small opening well off the ground—which suggests that it was deliberately placed there (for votive purposes again?) after the eruption but before the destruction of the palace and thus implies that some time had elapsed between the two events.

Whatever the date of the eruption, it should be obvious from the foregoing discussion that nature alone, even with a combination of ashfall, tsunamis, and earthquakes within a relatively short period, cannot fully account for the destruction, especially since the destruction of the palaces and mansions was, more often than not, accomplished by or at least completed by fire. Earthquakes can cause fires, by upsetting oil lamps or pots of oil on cooking fires, but they do not invariably do so. The frequency of fire involved in the destruction on Crete suggests deliberate arson.[41]

Could it be that the Minoans were economically weakened and perhaps demoralized by the physical and psychological damage done by their traumatic experience to such an extent that some emigrated while those who remained were constantly harassed by marauders who took advantage of the confusion, and that eventually the Mycenaeans wrested power from the ruler at Knossos and systematically destroyed the other palaces and mansions to forestall any potential challenge to their authority? If an earthquake happened to have occurred while the Minoans were still recovering from the immediate effects of the eruption not far from their shores (ashfall certainly, tsunamis rather probably), that would have made them all the more vulnerable.[42]

If the natural catastrophe was not directly responsible for the demise of Minoan civilization, does that completely rule out Crete as the prototype of Atlantis? If Plato is to be taken seriously, yes. Insistence on the reality of the Egyptian document forces us back to Frost's original suggestion, that the sudden cessation of trade just looked to the Egyptians as though Crete had sunk without trace. But under our third alternative, that Plato invented Atlantis to make a philosophical point (as he invented other myths), there is room for the possibility that for some of the details in his description he could have called upon his knowledge of the geography of Crete and whatever he knew of the (to him) mythical civilization, centered around a labyrinthine palace at Knossos where the bull (the Minotaur) figured prominently. Have not authors everywhere and in all ages drawn upon their own experience and knowledge in creating characters, places, and situations? In using a real setting, Plato would nevertheless have been perfectly free to blow up the dimensions of his mythical island kingdom and move it to the more commodious and more mysterious oceanic location. It also would have been quite natural to him to picture his seafaring Atlanteans as worshipping the sea god, whose symbol was the bull.

There is one detail of his description of Atlantean customs, the ritual involving the sacrifice of netted bulls, which is so startlingly close to scenes depicted on Minoan artifacts that it seems to suggest that Plato himself may have gotten the idea from such a representation, perhaps without even knowing the true provenance of what in his time would already have been an object of great antiquity. But on the other hand, how else but with a strong net would one go about capturing a large dangerous animal alive and unhurt? This method is still used today, in taking wild animals for zoos or for scientific study and release.

So far as we know, no mention of the Bronze Age eruption of Santorini appears to have survived until Plato's time in recognizable form, even in legend. Considering that the eruption was a fact and that it undoubtedly was one of the most spectacular events in the Aegean in prehistoric times, clearly visible from parts of Crete and having repercussions in many other places (sound waves, shock waves, ashfall, tsunamis, blackouts or dimouts attendant on the great amounts of ash in the atmosphere), this is indeed surprising. Possibly some oral tradition concerning it survived to Plato's time but has died out since. But it is not really necessary for him to have been aware of the collapse of Santorini to have imagined a watery grave for Atlantis. What easier way is there—in fiction, though not in fact—to destroy an island than to plunge it beneath the waves?

Having considered the various possibilities, let us return to the original question—is Atlantis myth or legend? I have tried to show that an Atlantic site, and with it a literal interpretation of Plato's description, is ruled out by our present knowledge of the sea floors. With one exception, alternative sites fail to provide both of the essential elements of the Atlantis story, a powerful and advanced civilization destroyed by a natural catastrophe. As for the exception, the effects of the Santorini eruption, when viewed realistically from the geologic point of view, cannot wholly account for the destruction of Minoan Crete even if that eruption occurred very shortly before or was essentially simultaneous with the destruction, and there is some indication that it actually occurred some fifty years earlier.

The very best we can do is to grant that Plato might have derived some of his ideas from Minoan Crete in one way or another, but such a derivation is far too roundabout for Atlantis to qualify as a legend which presents a distorted view of an actual event. From the geological point of view, I fear that Atlantis must be considered just another of the myths of Plato.

II. Glacial Fluctuations, Sea-level Changes, and Catastrophic Floods

HERBERT E. WRIGHT, JR.

According to Plato's account, Atlantis was suddenly submerged beneath the sea 9,000 years before the time of Solon, that is, about 11,600 years ago. Ever since the expansive treatment of the Atlantis question by Ignatius Donnelly a century ago, various geological processes have been evoked to explain this catastrophe. Emphasis has been placed on volcanic eruptions, earthquakes, and other disruptions of the earth. These types of catastrophe are known from historic time, and they can be inferred for the past from the discovery of marine fossils far above the sea and of terrestrial objects (like tree trunks) now submerged. With the development of geological concepts of continental drift in the 1920s, many writers proposed the widening of the Atlantic Ocean and the subsidence of a landmass. But usually the geological evidence is cited out of context, with little regard for the time scale, and outlandish arguments are evoked to support a favorite story of catastrophic submergence—not only for Atlantis but for the even greater continent of Mu in the mid-Pacific.

The magnitude and chronology of geological processes are better understood today than in the days of Donnelly. Volcanic explosions and local crustal collapses that often accompany these events are well documented. The "tidal waves" associated with collapses or earthquakes in oceanic areas affect coastal regions far away, and they are certainly sudden enough to qualify as catastrophes. The scientific documentation of the magnitude and chronology of the explosion and collapse of Santorini in the Aegean Sea establishes this locale as a leading contender for Atlantis. The recent increase in geological knowledge about continental drift and the opening of the Atlantic Ocean, however, provides no clues for the fate of Atlantis, for the process is much too slow to be catastrophic, and the magnitude of the crustal change in the few thousand years involved is negligible.

Another geological approach to the submergence of Atlantis requires a catastrophic rise in sea level rather than a subsidence of the land. This is the proposition with which I shall deal in the remainder of this essay.

Of all the inexorable earth forces that might menace man on a global scale, glaciation is one of the most impressive in the popular mind. The extent of Ice-Age glaciation in the northern hemisphere was impressively large, and the effects of the glacial climate on the animal life of peripheral regions are attested by the famous paintings of reindeer in the limestone caves in southern France. Moreover, it is easy for laymen to understand that the source of moisture for clouds and thus for the snow that nourished ice sheets is the oceans, and that as glaciers advance the sea level must drop. Conversely, they appreciate the threat that the sea level must rise as the glaciers retreat, causing submergence of coastal areas, where much of the human population has lived throughout history.

Many people are apprehensive today that industrial air pollution can affect the world climate and cause the great ice sheets to advance, bringing about a change in the economy of the northern countries. They are also told that air pollution might instead have the reverse effect—bringing about the retreat of glaciers and the inundation of coastal cities. The idea is reinforced by three recent findings suggesting that Ice-Age glaciation was caused by very slight climatic changes. First, analysis of sediment cores from the deep ocean basins indicates that the temperature differences of ocean surface waters between cold times and warm times was only 4–6°F. Second, studies of the modern climate in northeastern Canada, where the last North American ice sheet originated, suggest that a decrease in summer temperature of a very few degrees could result in widespread persistence of snow patches throughout the summer; the gradual accumulation of snow year after year could result in the thickening and merging of snow patches until an ice sheet was formed simultaneously over a very broad area. And third, weather records for the last hundred years indicate a fluctuation of at least 1°F in average annual temperature; larger changes in the past are suggested by historic records of great storminess and expansion of sea ice in the North Atlantic, by expansion of glaciers in Alaska and the Alps, and by other events whose climatic implications are clear although not easily quantified. With predictions that thermal discharges from nuclear power plants, along with industrial air pollution, will change the atmospheric heat budget and thereby affect the regime of glaciers, we have the setting for popular ideas of catastrophic effects of modern civilization.

But even without consideration of modern man's influence on climate, the elements necessary to envision catastrophic effects on ancient man are there. Some writers are thus tempted to exploit ice sheets and climatic change as scapegoats for cultural events that cannot otherwise easily be explained. Others appeal to natural forces such as these as the basis for legends involving catastrophic events. This is the category in which the Atlantis story can be placed.

A major advantage of the glacial theory for sea-level rise to explain the submergence of Atlantis is the chronology. According to Plato's account, Atlantis was lost 11,600 years ago, and this is precisely the time that is often mentioned as the end of the last glacial period, when the ice sheets melted and returned their water to the sea. Most of the problems in correlating glacial and sea-level changes with cultural events, however, come from an inadequate understanding of either the time scale or the rates of natural processes. The following review shows that the natural process of glacial advance and retreat is so slow that global flooding fast enough to qualify as a catastrophe is just not part of the picture.

There is little question but that sea level was depressed during the glacial period far below its present level. The generally accepted figure of 350 feet is based on two lines of evidence—calculated volumes of the several ice sheets, which were made from snow that could come only from moisture evaporated from the oceans, and the finding of terrestrial or shallow-water fossils at depths submerged during the postglacial rise in sea level.[1] The areas of the ancient ice sheets are fairly accurately known from maps of glacial deposits, and the thickness is assumed to be similar to that of the present-day Greenland ice sheet—about 10,000 feet in the center. The volume of water thus calculated should result in the lowering of sea level by 450 feet. But removal of the load of water from the ocean basin should cause the uplift of the oceanic crust by one-third this amount, because the earth's crust tends to maintain a balance, and the mass of a unit volume of water is about one-third that of crustal rocks. So the net sea-level depression at the time of maximal glaciation is about 350 rather than 450 feet.

The ice sheets reached their maximal extent about 18,000 years ago. The front of the North American ice sheet extended from the New York City area westward to southern Illinois, thence northwestward across the plains to the Canadian Rocky Mountains, where it merged with a less extensive mountain ice sheet. In Europe, the Scandinavian ice sheet was much smaller; it extended southward to Denmark and the capitals of eastern Europe—Berlin, Warsaw, and Moscow—and in the North Sea it was joined by a still smaller ice cap from the British Isles. Ice caps covered the Alps and other mountains of more southerly latitudes. In the southern hemisphere the only ice sheet was in Argentina, extending east from the Andes.

Retreat of the ice sheets from 18,000 to about 11,000 years ago was presumably a response to climatic change, but it was marked by numerous fluctuations. The position of an ice front is determined by an equilibrium among three principal factors: (1) the accumulation of snow, centered well back from the ice margin, (2) the velocity of ice flow outward from the accumulation area, and (3) wastage of the ice margin by melting or by the breaking off of icebergs where the glacier meets the sea or a deep lake. If these factors are balanced for many hundreds of years, the continued internal flow of the ice to the margin transports rock fragments eroded from the glacier bed. During melting these rock fragments are deposited at the ice front in the form of a moraine. Inception of a warmer climate causes the ice front to melt back to a new equilibrium position. In Illinois, for example, a series of climatic fluctuations during general ice retreat is recorded by about thirty moraines formed during the interval from 18,000 to 14,000 years ago. Fluctuations of greater magnitude but less frequency occurred in other ice lobes protruding from the ice sheet in the Great Lakes area.

After about 11,000 years ago the ice front retreated more rapidly. Part of the increased pace reflects the fact that the perimeter of the ice sheet had been reduced substantially by this time and the thickness was less, so that not so much ice had to be melted for every mile of ice retreat. But independent evidence from pollen studies of vegetational history indicates that climatic warming accelerated about this time.[2] What had been a widespread spruce forest throughout most of the central and eastern United States for many thousands of years changed rather abruptly to forests of pine or mixed hardwoods much like those of today. A similar sequence is documented for Europe, where the tundra vegetation of the glacial period was rapidly transformed to pine-birch forests and then to hardwoods. The climate 9,000 years ago on both continents was much like the modern climate, even though the ice sheets were still present to the north. The lag in ice-sheet retreat, especially in North America, is a tribute to the huge reservoir of ice that had to be melted. The ice did not clear Hudson Bay until after 8,000 years ago, and a few residual masses lasted in northeastern Canada until the present day.

The retreat of the ice front should be matched by the rise of sea level, because water stored in the ice sheet was returned to the sea.[3] The curve for sea-level rise is based on the radiocarbon dates of organic matter (wood, shells) found buried in the coastal sediments at various depths. The organic material must be of a type that grew close to the sea level of the day. Sea-level curves have been constructed for many coastal areas (for example, Florida, Massachusetts, Netherlands, certain Pacific islands, Brazil). They all show that the rise of sea level was grossly similar in all areas, from a low of 350 feet 18,000 years ago to a level close to that of the present about 5,000 years ago. Some curves purport to show significant changes within the last 5,000 years, correlated with minor glacial fluctuations and paleoclimatic trends, but it is difficult to distinguish changes of a few feet in average sea level from the effects of occasional hurricanes, tidal waves, and strong wind storms.

If the glacial fluctuations were synchronous from lobe to lobe—a reasonable supposition if they were caused by regional climatic changes—then an interval of ice advance should be recorded by a temporary drop in sea level and thus by a nick in the curve for sea-level rise. Unfortunately, the dating control on the sea-level curve is not sufficiently detailed to check this proposition. In fact, the assumption of synchronous lobe fluctuations is not well supported by radiocarbon dates of moraines, nor is it supported by independent evidence for climatic fluctuations during the period of ice retreat.

For example, one classification of the last glaciation is based on the history of the Lake Michigan ice lobe. It emphasizes an episode of ice retreat (the Two Creeks interval) about 12,000 years ago followed by ice advance of about 150 miles. It has been shown that adjacent ice lobes did not advance at the same time, and the pollen record of vegetational history provides no evidence for significant climatic fluctuation at this time.

So at this point we are left with a picture of a slowly retreating ice front and a slowly rising sea level over many thousands of years, with possible fluctuations whose magnitude and chronology are not well delineated. Correlating a catastrophic event in cultural history that lasted at most a few decades—whether fact or legend—with the entire period of sea-level rise, or even with a single fluctuation, therefore has no basis because the time scale of the natural events is so long.

The most recent effort to implicate glaciers in the legends of floods and similar catastrophes attempts to introduce some speed into the glacial process and thus into the rate of sea-level rise. It was made in *Science*, a prestigious scientific journal, by a group of geochemists and marine scientists at the University of Miami.[4] They found evidence in the sediments of the Gulf of Mexico that the seawater had temporarily freshened at a time they placed at 11,600 years ago. Adopting the recent suggestion that the advance of ice lobes in the basins of Lake Michigan, Lake Superior, and Lake Winnipeg about this time may have resulted from a sudden surge of the ice rather than a normal climatic fluctuation, they propose that an equally rapid melting of the distended ice lobes introduced a great flood of meltwater into the Mississippi River and thence the Gulf of Mexico. They postulate not only that the seawater was freshened by the influx of meltwater but that sea level rose the world around by a foot or so per year. They conclude that this event "could be an explanation for the deluge stories common to many Eurasian, Australasian, and American traditions," including the account of Plato, who set the date at 9,000 years before Solon, or 11,600 years before the present.

The account in *Science* was duly reported in a serious vein in the national and international press. It requires close scrutiny because it purports to apply carefully acquired quantitative scientific data in an ingenious way to an age-old problem in literary history. Classicists who have tried to fathom the meaning of Plato's account, however, should not rush to accept this explanation, for the validity of the scientific argument may be questioned every step of the way.

A glacial surge is a rapid advance of the outer part of a glacier or ice lobe to a distended position well beyond its normal equilibrium extent. It does not reflect a change in the balance between snow accumulation and wastage, but rather an abrupt change in the physical factors controlling ice flow. Ice flow is controlled by many factors, of which the most important is probably the temperature at the base of the ice. If the ice is cold and frozen to the rock beneath, then ice flow is primarily within the ice itself. But if the basal ice is at the melting point, then water can exist at the rock surface and the sliding friction of the glacier is greatly reduced. The temperature of the ice depends in turn on several factors: (1) the heat input from the air, and thus the climate, (2) heat input from the earth's crust, and thus the nature of the rock beneath the ice, (3) rate of snow accumulation, and thus the rate of compaction and downward flow of cold ice to the base, and (4) friction of ice flow, and thus the flow velocity. Most of these factors are dynamic, and they combine in various ways to result in temperature profiles through the ice that can change with time. It is possible that a frozen condition at the base of much of an ice lobe could pass to an unfrozen condition, greatly increasing the velocity of flow.

At the same time, the terminus of the ice lobe might tend to remain frozen to the base for a longer period—the ice is thinner and less plastic, and the presence of a lot of rock debris inhibits ice flow and thus the production of frictional heat. The terminus might then provide a kind of dam for the accelerated ice flow from the main portion of the lobe. Eventually, however, the dam might give way as the ice piles up behind, and the entire mass then surges forward until it becomes too thin to flow any more even with the reduced friction at the base. It then freezes to its bed once again, and the stagnant distended portion, being beyond the normal equilibrium limit, rapidly wastes away.

Although the Miami authors present no calculations, their evidence for the magnitude of the ice-sheet fluctuation at 11,600 years ago is apparently a curve showing ice-sheet areas at various times during the general glacial retreat.[5] On this curve and the accompanying table, the ice advance 11,600 years ago is shown as a 2 percent change in area. A normal ice-sheet fluctuation caused by climatic change involves a proportionate change in sea level, because the water comes from the sea and must be returned thereto. A sea level change of 2 percent would amount to about eight feet, which might be enough to notice on coastal areas if it occurred within a few years.

Two problems come with the 2 percent, however. The first problem has to do with the ice areas involved in the 11,600-year-ago advance. Recent study of the glacial deposits of the Lake Michigan lobe and of the deposits of the large proglacial lake in front of the ice indicate that the glacial advance assigned to 11,600 years ago occurred instead about 13,000 years ago, and that the one at 11,600 was appreciably smaller.[6] Furthermore, significant ice advances in the Lake Superior and Winnipeg areas, whether they be surges or not, occurred long before or after 11,600 years ago and are therefore not relevant to the question; outflow from proglacial lakes in the Superior and Winnipeg basins did feed into the Mississippi River and involved large discharges of water, but there is no basis for identifying a sudden increase in outflow 11,600 years ago.

If the Superior and Winnipeg lobes are eliminated from consideration, and if the case then rests on the smaller of the two Lake Michigan lobe advances, then the postulated 2 percent change of the ice volume and water volume involved in a possible surge and subsequent melting would be cut to a third or less, and the rise of sea level then would not be eight feet but only, say, two feet.

The second problem with accepting an eight-foot figure is that if a surge was involved the advance of an ice lobe does not necessarily mean a proportionate change in sea level. A surge involves no change in ice volume—only ice area. The lobe simply advances by thinning; no more water is extracted from the sea to make snow. The Miami authors assume, however, that the distended ice lobe should melt very rapidly, being beyond the normal terminus, and that such melting is the cause of the sea-level rise. This proposition can be evaluated in the following way.

If the Lake Michigan lobe surged halfway down the basin, the lake at its front would be partly displaced, and the water would be decanted into the Mississippi River by way of the Chicago River. Rough calculation of the volume of water decanted shows that ocean volume would increase by about .0002 percent, so the total rise in sea level would be a tiny fraction of an inch.

The rate of rise of sea level under these circumstances would depend on the rate of advance of the surging ice lobe, plus the capacity of the outlet to accommodate the decanted outflow. The rate of advance of a surging ice lobe is impossible to determine. Surges of the Rocky Mountain glaciers last only a few years at most, but the glaciers are so much smaller than the Lake Michigan lobe that the comparison is not really valid. A forest was apparently overridden, and the outer rings of the tree trunks show a narrowing that is attributed to a rise in lake level as the ice approached the site. If this interpretation is correct, the ice advance lasted for several years, and the decantation of the proglacial lake lasted equally long. If the surge lasted for twenty years, the decantation would cause sea level to rise an even tinier fraction of an inch per year for this period—hardly a catastrophe in human terms.

The water volumes involved might be greater if the surge was preceded by a substantial damming of ice behind a frozen toe. Under these conditions basal water could build up beneath the ice for many hundreds of years, because it could not escape through the impermeable frozen toe. Sometimes such dammed-up water can escape in discrete channels, which cut deep gorges in the substratum beneath the ice.[7] But if it remains as a thin sheet beneath the ice it simply increases until the sliding friction of the ice is reduced even more, and eventually the ice mass slides forward over or through the dam as a surge. The stored basal water thereby released would be added to the water in the proglacial lake, thus increasing the decant down the Mississippi River.

Although the release of stored water might be a phenomenon in a glacial surge, the actual volume of water is not significant in the problem. It is usually calculated that the water film involved at the base of a glacier is only a small fraction of an inch thick, so the amount of water contributed to a proglacial lake of about the same area would be insignificant.

Actually, the Miami group did not appeal to decantation as the mechanism for sea-level rise, but rather to the accelerated melting of the distended portion of the surged ice lobe. To evaluate this explanation, we can first calculate the total effect of the melting on sea level, and then consider how the rate of melting might occasion a catastrophe.

The volume of the distended ice lobe must first be estimated. Before the time of surging, the ice front had withdrawn to the northern end of Lake Michigan, to allow the drainage of lake beds on which the forest grew. The ice then surged halfway down the Lake Michigan basin, a distance of about 150 miles, and it spilled over into the northern part of the Lake Huron basin as well. The marginal part of the ice sheet that surged may have had an average thickness of 3,000 feet, depending on how far back into the main ice sheet the effect occurred. After surging, the ice was thinner, of course—perhaps less than 2,000 feet on the average. With such a figure the volume of the distended lobe can be estimated. Once melted, this volume of ice could raise sea level by a very small fraction of 1 percent. Sea level at the time was about 150 feet below the present level. It had been rising at an average rate of about a half-inch per year for several thousand years. With the melting of the surged ice lobe, the additional increase would be only a very few inches. Even if surges in the Lake Superior and

Lake Winnipeg lobes were included, as in the original proposition, the sea-level rise would not be much more.

As far as the rate for the sea-level rise is concerned, instantaneous melting of a surged ice lobe cannot be assumed. Melting rates for stagnant ice depend on the amount of rock debris in the ice, among other factors. As the ice melts down from the surface, the rock debris becomes concentrated at the surface and forms a mantle that protects the underlying ice from further rapid melting. The debris-covered ice may survive for hundreds of years. Stagnant ice originally about 700 feet thick resulting from a glacial surge in the mountains of the Yukon still exists 1,200 years after its emplacement, even though the ice contains less than 2 percent rock debris.[8] There is evidence in Minnesota that stagnant ice in some of the early moraines lasted for as much as 9,000 years, virtually until the end of the glacial period.[9]

Even if the distended ice were devoid of rock debris, melting could hardly have been catastrophic. Not only must heat be supplied to warm the ice to melting temperature, but very much more heat is necessary to convert the ice to water. Rough calculations show that with the amount of solar radiation available in the melt season at the latitude of Lake Michigan, supplemented by warm rains and winds, it would take many decades to melt 2,000 feet of clean ice. The annual rate of sea-level rise thus becomes almost infinitesimally small, even when a protective dirt mantle does not form.

Now if we look at the other link in the story—the geochemical evidence from cores in the Gulf of Mexico—we can also challenge the conclusions. The evidence involves the ratio of two isotopes of oxygen—0^{18} and 0^{16}—in the calcium carbonate shells of Foraminifera. These little animals live in great abundance in the surface waters of the sea, and the isotopic composition of their shells reflects the temperature and isotopic composition of the water. When seawater evaporates to form water vapor, more 0^{16} goes into the vapor, leaving 0^{18} behind. During the glacial period much of this 0^{16}-rich water vapor fell as snow and ended up in ice sheets.

When the ice sheets melted and returned the water to the sea, the isotopic ratio in the seawater returned to its nonglacial mode.

Analyses of oxygen-isotope ratios in sediment cores from the Gulf of Mexico indicate an abrupt peak in the 0^{16} content at a level dated by the Miami investigators as centering around 11,600 years ago. But each of the samples dated by radiocarbon analysis included at least 1,350 years of sediment, and the statistical error in each date amounts to at least 140 years. This all means that assigning a date of precisely 11,600 years ago is not justified. A more conservative interpretation of the results indicates that the peak covers the time span 12,550 to 11,200 years ago—a span of 1,350 years, which is certainly not a catastrophic change in cultural terms.

Furthermore, similar analyses of other cores in the Gulf of Mexico by other investigators imply different times for the freshwater influx, and certainly not times of short span.[10] The core with the most detail suggests a range of 17,000 to 12,000 years ago for the interval of freshwater influx, roughly equivalent to the entire time of ice retreat in the Great Lakes region, with the peak occurring 14,000 to 12,000 years ago. After that time the discharge from the melting ice lobes shifted to the east to the Atlantic Ocean by way of the Hudson and St. Lawrence rivers. The other two cores, with less detailed analyses, imply dates of 20,000 to 15,000 and 12,000 to 10,000 years ago—perhaps an indication of the imprecision in dating ocean-sediment cores. A more conservative interpretation of the oxygen-isotope studies in the Gulf of Mexico correlates the high values in the oxygen-isotope curves with the entire interval of wastage of all the ice lobes in the Mississippi River drainage system—an interval from roughly 18,000 to 11,500 years ago.

The relation of the oxygen-isotope record to meltwater influx is not disputed. The change in isotope ratios is distinct and significant, at least in one or two of the four cores studied. But a corresponding change in sea level is not required by the oxygen results, which pertain only to surface waters. The fresh water from the Mississippi River floats on the surface, where most of the foraminiferans live. Deeper-water forms did not show such a large change in isotope ratios.

In conclusion, there seems little support on the geological side to attribute the submergence of Atlantis 11,600 years ago to a rise of sea level related to glacial events. Sea level had already been rising for thousands of years by this time and was due to rise another 150 feet before approaching its present level about 5,000 years ago. Slight but undetectable changes in rates of sea-level rise probably occurred as an effect of minor climatic changes on the regime of the ice sheets, but the lack of exact synchroneity in the advances and retreats of the various ice lobes and ice sheets throughout the world probably tended to dampen such abrupt changes that might otherwise have been recorded. The postulated 2 percent change in ice area about 12,000 years ago is probably overemphasized. Glaciers are not immediate universal sensors of climatic change: an increase in snowfall in the interior of an ice sheet, for example, is not recorded by an advance of the ice front until a wave of ice flow has a chance to progress from the accumulation area to the terminus, and this can take tens or perhaps hundreds of years in the case of a long glacier. Surges of individual ice lobes are a somewhat different matter, but their effect on global sea level is negligible because the volumes of ice are relatively small and because melting is not immediate.

In view of the numerous difficulties in relating glacial events to short-term global sea-level changes, Atlantists will have to look elsewhere for their catastrophes.

Notes

Perspectives Ancient and Modern

1. L. S. de Camp, *Lost Continents: The Atlantis Theme in History and Literature* (New York, 1954; Dover ed., 1970). De Camp has an extensive bibliography of Atlantis literature at the end of his book. For other surveys, see p. 197 below.
2. The Apaturia was an Athenian festival held late in the year, on the last day of which the children, young men, and new wives were inducted into the phratries or brotherhoods.
3. For a summary of what is known about the Palaeolithic and Mesolithic periods in the Eastern Mediterranean, see S. S. Weinberg, "The Stone Age in the Aegean," *Cambridge Ancient History*[3], vol. 1, part 1, pp. 557–65.
4. Tacitus, *Germania* 17.
5. Plutarch, *Moralia* 941A–B.
6. [Skylax], *Periplous* 112.
7. Aristotle, *On Meteorology* 2.1.354a.
8. Herodotus, *History* 2.102.
9. Avienus, *Description of the World* 57–61; *Maritime Shores* 406–15.
10. Strabo, *Geography* 2.102; 13.598.
11. Proclus, *Commentary on Plato's Timaeus* 24A (ed. Diehl).
12. Strabo, *Geography* 2.102.
13. Pliny the Elder, *Natural History* 2.92.205.
14. Philo Judaeus, *On the Eternity of the World* 26.141.
15. Diodorus Siculus, *World History* 3.54.1–6; 3.56–61.
16. Plutarch, *Life of Solon* 26.1.
17. Tertullian, *On the Ascetics' Mantle* 2; *Apology* 40.4.
18. Athenaeus, *Deipnosophists* 14.640e.
19. Aelian, *On the Characteristics of Animals* 15.2.

20. Ammianus Marcellinus, *Roman History* 17.7.13.
21. Proclus, *Commentary on Timaeus* 55A.
22. Proclus, *Commentary on Timaeus* 24B–D.
23. Proclus, *Commentary on Timaeus* 24A.
24. Cosmas Indicopleustes, *Christian Topography* 12.456D (ed. Winstedt; see also 12.453A–B). The mistakes Cosmas makes with Plato's story and the Christian overtones that he adds to it make his account quite interesting.
25. De Camp (above, note 1), p. 22.
26. T. Henri Martin, *Études sur le Timée* (Paris, 1841), vol. 1, p. 272.
27. De Camp (above, note 1), pp. 314–18 provides a list of people and their conjectures.
28. Martin (above, note 26), 2 vols. His discussion of Atlantis appears in volume 1, pp. 257–333.
29. Martin (above, note 26), vol. 1, pp. 330–32.
30. Ignatius Donnelly, *Atlantis: The Antediluvian World* (New York, 1882). This has appeared in many reprintings and in a second edition edited by Egerton Sykes (New York, 1949). References in the notes which follow are to Sykes' edition.
31. De Camp (above, note 1), p. 42.
32. Donnelly (above, note 30), p. 111.
33. Donnelly (above, note 30), pp. 230-38.
34. Donnelly (above, note 30), pp. 157-58.
35. De Camp (above, note 1), p. 91. Lewis Spence, *The Problem of Atlantis* (New York, 1924: 2nd ed. 1925).
36. Lewis Spence, *The History of Atlantis* (London, 1926; New York, 1968), p. 88. References here and below are to the 1968 edition.
37. I. Velikovsky, *Worlds in Collision* (Garden City, N.Y., 1950). See also his *Earth in Upheaval* (New York, 1955).
38. On the effect of tsunamis see D. B. Vitaliano, *Legends of the Earth* (Bloomington, Ind., 1973), pp. 100–101, 146–50, 192–94, and her essay below, pp. 149–51.
39. Charles Schuchert, "Atlantis and the Permanency of the North Atlantic Ocean Bottom," *Proceedings of the National Academy of Sciences* 3 (1917), 65–72.
40. See also Vitaliano (above, note 38), pp. 223–29.
41. C. Emiliani *et al.*, "Paleoclimatological Analysis of Late Quaternary Cores from the Northeastern Gulf of Mexico," *Science* 189 (1975), 1083–88.
42. The cups are pictured in R. Higgins, *Minoan and Mycenaean Art*

(New York, 1967), figures 178–80 on pages 145–46. On the Santorini-Crete hypothesis see J. V. Luce, *The End of Atlantis* (U.S.A. title: *Lost Atlantis*) (London and New York, 1969) and Vitaliano (above, note 38), pp. 179–271.

43. For example, Higgins (above, note 42), p. 18, and N. Platon, *Zakros: The Discovery of a Lost Palace of Ancient Crete* (New York, 1971), pp. 303–20.
44. Schuchert (above, note 39), p. 71. On tachylite see also Vitaliano (above, note 38), pp. 223–24, and her essay below, pp. 141–42.
45. W. D. Matthew, "Plato's Atlantis in Palaeogeography," *Proceedings of the National Academy of Sciences* 6 (1920), 17.
46. G. C. Vaillant, review of A. Braghine, *The Shadow of Atlantis, Natural History* 45 (1940), 313.
47. G. C. Vaillant, *The Aztecs of Mexico* (New York, 1944; Penguin ed., 1950), p. 37.
48. L. D. Leet, *Causes of Catastrophe* (New York, 1948), pp. 215, 219–20.
49. H. E. Wright, letter to the editor of *Science* dated October 15, 1975, and circulated privately. His views are elaborated in his essay below, pp. 166–74.
50. Spence (above, note 36), p. 2.

The Sources and Literary Form of Plato's Atlantis Narrative

1. B. Jowett, *The Dialogues of Plato* (Oxford, 1892), vol. 3, p. 519.
2. J. A. Stewart, *The Myths of Plato* (London, 1905), p. 466.
3. A. E. Taylor, *A Commentary on Plato's Timaeus* (Oxford, 1928), p. 50; F. M. Cornford, *Plato's Cosmology* (London, 1937), pp. 8, 18.
4. A. Rivaud, *Platon, oeuvres complètes: Timée, Critias*[10] (Paris, 1925), p. 12.
5. Rivaud (above, note 4), pp. 30–31 (editor's translation).
6. P. Frutiger, *Les mythes de Platon* (Paris, 1930), pp. 245, 193–94 (editor's translation).
7. See *Laws* 713b–e for a similar treatment of the myth of Kronos and the Golden Age.
8. Theophrastus, *Doctrines of Natural Philosophers,* fragment 12 (H. Diehls, *Doxographi Graeci,* p. 490, 5–9); Posidonius in Strabo, *Geography* 2.102.
9. G. Stallbaum, *Platonis opera omnia recensuit et commentariis instruxit* (Gotha, 1827–1860), on *Timaeus* 24e: "Sed non est pro-

fecto cur Platonem dubitemus revera usum esse fontibus alienis, (hoc est, Aegyptiis), unde hauserit hanc narrationem." ("But there is certainly no reason to doubt that Plato really did use foreign sources [that is, Egyptian ones] from which he drew this account.") (editor's translation). T. H. Martin, *Études sur le Timée de Platon* (Paris, 1841), vol. 1, p. 332.

10. G. Grote, *Plato and the Other Companions of Socrates* (London, 1865), vol. 3, pp. 295 note, 299. H. Berger, article "Atlantis" in Pauly-Wissowa, *Realenzyclopädie der classischen Altertumswissenschaft*, vol. 4, col. 2118 (editor's translation).
11. L. Robin, "Platon et la science sociale," *Revue de metaphysique et de morale* 21 (1913), 219–21; J. B. Skemp, *Plato's Statesman* (London, 1952), p. 85.
12. Proclus, *Commentary on Timaeus* 24D.
13. Proclus, *Commentary on Timaeus* 24E. Compare 26E: the legend "contributes to the whole ensemble of the doctrine of nature." Compare also 40B and 61A.
14. Cornford (above, note 3), p. 1.
15. W. Brandenstein, *Grösse und Untergang eines geheimnisvolle Inselreiches* (Vienna, 1951), pp. 40–42, 49, also insists that Plato would not have sought to confirm his Ideal State with a concrete example which was fictitious and indeed could not have done so, as the literary genre of the fictitious "True History" had not yet appeared.
16. *Timaeus* 27b, translated by Cornford. Compare *Timaeus* 26d.
17. In making Timaeus describe his discourse as a "reasonable story" (*eikos muthos: Timaeus* 29d), Plato is indulging in ironical depreciation. Similarly in making Socrates call the Atlantis legend a "true account" (*alethes logos: Timaeus* 26e), he is indulging in ironical eulogy. These playful touches should not be allowed to obscure his intention to present the contents of both dialogues as possessing a similar status. See further the penetrating remarks of L. Edelstein, "The Function of Myth in Plato's Philosophy," *Journal of the History of Ideas* 10 (1949), 467, on the similar presuppositions governing Plato's presentation of cosmogonic and prehistoric events. Also, pp. 469–70, on the "pastime" (*paidia*—Platonic irony again) of collecting stories and composing them to a pattern.
18. Grote (above, note 10), vol. 3, p. 285.
19. Long span of time: *Timaeus* 22b–d; *Laws* 676b. Loss of records:

Timaeus 20e; 23a–b; *Critias* 109d–e; *Laws* 682b–c. Periodic disasters: *Timaeus* 22d–e; *Laws* 677a.

20. R. Weil, *L' "Archéologie" de Platon* (Paris, 1959). Weil mentions only two earlier writers who devoted systematic work to Plato as a historian: G. Rohr, *Platons Stellung zur Geschichte* (Berlin, 1932); K. I. Bourberis, *Hai historikai gnoseis tou Platonos* (Athens, 1938).
21. G. B. Kerferd, review of R. Weil, *L' 'Archeologie' de Platon, Classical Review* 11 (1961), 30–31; C. H. Kahn, review of Weil, *Classical Philology* 57 (1962), 118.
22. G. R. Morrow, *Plato's Cretan City: A Historical Interpretation of the Laws* (Princeton, 1960), p. 10.
23. *Republic* 595a–608b. Compare *Republic* 382d on the inevitability of *pseudos* in mythology.
24. Morrow (above, note 22), p. 72.
25. Kahn (above, note 21), p. 118.
26. For the Atlantis narrative as a *logos*, see *Timaeus* 20d; 21a; 21c; 21d; 26e; 27b; *Critias* 108c.
27. Paneguris (festival) of the goddess, *Timaeus* 21a; compare 26e. "Exploits" and "encomium," *Timaeus* 20e–21a; *Critias* 108c.
28. See, for example, Isocrates, *Panegyricus* 68–70; *Archidamus* 42; *Areopagiticus* 75; *Panathenaicus* 191–95. Lysias, *Epitaphios* 3–16.
29. *Critias* 106c–108a. For a similar plea, see Lysias, *Epitaphios* 1–2.
30. Lineage of the prehistoric Athenians as autochthonous scions of Hephaestus and Athena: *Critias* 109d. Nurture and education: *Critias* 110c–d; 111b–d. Their exploits (by implication): *Critias* 112d–e. Roughly the same scheme may be traced in the account of the Atlanteans (*Critias* 113b–121c), particularly in the lineage of the kings in descent from Poseidon and Cleito (113c–114d). See further on this last point P. Friedländer, *Platon*² (Berlin, 1960), vol. 3, pp. 357-58, where suggestive comparisons and contrasts are drawn between the *Critias* and the *Menexenus*. I had worked out my point about the *Critias* as a *logos panegurikos* before reading this passage of Friedländer. What he says suggests my point without making it so explicit.
31. See further on this point pp. 71–72 below.
32. E. Diehl, *Anthologia Lyrica Graeca*³, fragment 6.
33. U. von Wilamowitz-Moellendorf, *Platon* (Berlin, 1948), vol. 1, pp. 242–45; J. Bidez, *Eos, ou Platon et l'Orient* (Brussels, 1945), pp. 21–22.
34. Wilamowitz (above, note 33), p. 244. Compare *Timaeus* 24a–c.

35. Proclus, *Commentary on Timaeus* 24A, reports, on the authority of Crantor, that Plato's contemporaries accused him of plagiarizing his Ideal State from Egyptian sources. Plato, Crantor continued, took the criticism seriously, and this explains his attribution of the Atlantis legend to Egyptian sources. The logic is not immediately obvious. The point appears to be as follows: The Atlantis story is documented for Plato by ancient Egyptian records and is therefore good testimony for the prehistory of *Athens*, and in particular for the existence of its *Republic*-type class structure. Plato could therefore guarantee, on the strength of Egyptian evidence, that the Ideal State was once a *Greek* reality. This explanation is taken from A. J. Festugière's edition of Proclus' *Commentary on the Timaeus* (Paris, 1966), vol. 1 [Book 1], p. 111, note 2. Compare the good remarks of Bidez (above, note 33), Appendix 2, p. 32.
36. Herodotus, *History* 2.142, where there is also the implication that the periodic reversals of the sun's orbit had caused destructions *elsewhere*. Plato develops this point in *Timaeus* 22d–e.
37. *Timaeus* 23e; *Critias* 108e. The same figure of 9,000 years is given in both passages, but in the former it apparently refers to the foundation of prehistoric Athens and in the latter to its war with Atlantis. This inconsistency is understandable, and would perhaps have been ironed out by Plato had he completed and revised the *Critias*.
38. For this ingenious hypothesis, see A. G. Galanopoulos and E. Bacon, *Atlantis: The Truth Behind the Legend* (London, 1969), pp. 133–34.
39. J. V. Luce, *The End of Atlantis* (U.S.A. title *Lost Atlantis*) (London and New York, 1969), p. 181.
40. R. O. Faulkner, "Egypt from the Inception of the Nineteenth Dynasty to the Death of Ramesses III," *Cambridge Ancient History*[3], vol. 2, part 2, pp. 230–31, 237.
41. See illustration 90 in Luce (above, note 39).
42. Festugière (above, note 35), vol. 1 [Book 1], p. 111.
43. *Timaeus* 21c. Plutarch, *Life of Solon* 31, disagrees, saying it was simply the onset of old age which deterred him.
44. P. Vidal-Naquet, "Athènes et l'Atlantide," *Revue des Études Grecques* 77 (1964), 428.
45. Herodotus, *History* 2.170. *Timaeus* 21e. For some interesting speculations on the Libyan and Minoan affiliations of Neïth-Athena, see A. J. Evans, *The Early Nilotic, Libyan and Egyptian Relations with Minoan Crete* (London, 1926), pp. 22–23. Evans emphasizes

the warlike attributes of the goddess, a point, we may note, also underlined by Plato (*Timaeus* 24b).

46. In an unsigned article in the *London Times* of February 19, 1909, and more fully in "The *Critias* and Minoan Crete," *Journal of Hellenic Studies* 33 (1913), 189–206; S. Marinatos, "Peri ton thrulon tes Atlantidos," *Kretika Chronika* 2 (1950), 195–213.
47. J. M. Cook, review of J. V. Luce, *The End of Atlantis, Classical Review* 20 (1970), 225.
48. S. Marinatos, "The Volcanic Destruction of Minoan Crete," *Antiquity* 13 (1939), 425–39.
49. A. Nicaise, *Thera, l'Atlantide et Krakatoa: Les terres disparues* (Paris, 1885); J. W. Mavor, *Voyage to Atlantis* (New York, 1969); Galanopoulos and Bacon (above, note 38).
50. D. L. Page, *The Santorini Volcano and the Destruction of Minoan Crete* (London, 1970), p. 12.
51. J. V. Luce, "Thera and the Devastation of Minoan Crete: A New Interpretation of the Evidence," *American Journal of Archaeology* 80 (1976), 9–16.
52. *Acta of the 1st International Scientific Congress on the Volcano of Thera, Greece, 1969* (Athens, 1971).
53. C. and D. Vitaliano, "Volcanic Tephra on Crete," *American Journal of Archaeology* 78 (1974), 19–24.
54. Bidez (above, note 33), Appendix 2. Compare P. Friedländer, *Plato*[2] (Princeton, 1969), vol. 1, pp. 319–20.
55. Compare Herodotus, *History* 1.98 and 1.178 with *Critias* 115c–119b.
56. C. Corbato, "In margine alla questione atlantidea. Platone e Cartagine," *Archeologia Classica* 5 (1953), 232–37.
57. *Scholia in Rempublicam* 327a (ed. Hermann, p. 331); Proclus, *Commentary on Timaeus* 26F. T. Gomperz, *Griechische Denker* (Leipzig, 1896), vol. 2, p. 604.
58. Brandenstein (above, note 15), pp. 60—61.
59. E. D. Phillips, "Historical Elements in the Myth of Atlantis," *Euphrosyne* 2 (1968), 36. Phillips in the rest of the article takes seriously, as I do, the Egyptian basis and the "Minoan hypothesis."
60. For the fragments of Hellanicus, see F. Jacoby, *Die Fragmente der griechischen Historiker* (Berlin, 1922–1958), vol. 1, A, 4; A. Lesky, *A History of Greek Literature*, transl. J. Willis and C. de Heer (London, 1966), p. 331.
61. Jacoby (above, note 60), IIIb (Supplement), vol. 1, pp. 1–11.

62. Hellanicus may have taken material from an earlier epic poem titled *Atlantis,* of which *Oxyrhynchus Papyri* 11, 1359 may be a fragment. See C. Robert, "Eine epische Atlantias," *Hermes* 52 (1917), 477–79.
63. Jacoby (above, note 60), vol. 1, A, 4, fragment 19b.
64. W. A. Heidel, "A Suggestion Concerning Plato's Atlantis," *Proceedings of the American Academy of Arts and Sciences* 68 (1933), 201. This article is useful for the geographical background of the Atlantis legend.
65. For ancient testimonies to this disaster, see the article "Helike" in Pauly-Wissowa, *Realenzyklopädie,* vol. 14, cols. 2855-58. Frutiger (above, note 6), p. 248, note 1, claimed to be the first to associate this event with the Atlantis narrative, but he was anticipated by Taylor (above, note 3), p. 56.
66. Pindar, *Paean* 4. 27–44. Plato's possible debt to this source is noted by H. Herter, "Altes und Neues zu Platons Kritias," *Rheinisches Museum* 92 (1944), 242. See also my discussion of the passage (above, note 39), pp. 118 ff., in relation to the Minoan trading post recently found on Kea and the Thera eruption.
67. Stewart (above, note 2), p. 405; Friedländer (above, note 54), vol. 1, pp. 202–203; Vidal-Naquet (above, note 44), pp. 433–43.
68. Vidal-Naquet (above, note 44), pp. 429–33. His paradoxical view is summed up in the statement (p. 429): "Rencontrant et vainquant l'Atlantide, qui donc vainc en réalité l'Athènes de Platon, sinon elle-même?" ("Whom, then, is the Athens of Plato really conquering other than herself, when she meets and conquers Atlantis?") (editor's translation.)
69. Aristotle, *Metaphysics* 1.2.982b.18: "the lover of myths is a kind of philosopher."

Plato's Atlantis: A Mythologist Looks at Myth

1. *Lost Continents*: *The Atlantis Theme in History, Science, and Literature* (New York, 1954; Dover ed., 1970), pp. 234, 235.
2. J. de Vries, *Forschungsgeschichte der Mythologie* (Munich, 1961), pp. 28–30; J. Ferguson, *Utopias of the Classical World* (Ithaca, N.Y., 1975), pp. 104–108.
3. For example, one will not find Euhemerism as a contemporary myth theory in R. Chase, *Quest for Myth* (Baton Rouge, La., 1949); P. Cohen, "Theories of Myth," *Man,* n.s.4 (1969), 337–53;

J. Peradotto, *Classical Mythology: An Annotated Bibliographical Survey* (Urbana, Ill., 1973). For Raglan's ideas, see F. R. S. Raglan, *The Hero* (New York, 1956).

4. D. B. Vitaliano, *Legends of the Earth: Their Geologic Origins* (Bloomington, Ind., 1973), p. 1; J. V. Luce, *The End of Atlantis* (U.S.A. title *Lost Atlantis*) (London and New York, 1969), p. 15.
5. It is the *positive* contribution of numbers and geometric forms to the overall meaning of *Timaeus* (in its entirety) and *Critias* which refutes Marinatos' ingenious suggestion (see A. G. Galanopoulos and E. Bacon, *Atlantis: The Truth Behind the Legend* [London, 1969], pp. 133–34), taken up by subsequent proponents (Luce [above, note 4], p. 181; Vitaliano [above, note 4], pp. 232–33), that the dimensions of both time and space in the description of Atlantis are ten times too large because of a scribal error with the Egyptian number system when the story was translated into Greek. There is no reason, however, to see "error" here at all when one takes into account the centrality of mathematics, especially geometry, to Plato's philosophy as a whole. See T. Heath, *A History of Greek Mathematics* (Oxford, 1921), vol. 1, pp. 284–315, especially p. 288: "We find in Plato's dialogues what appears to be the first serious attempt at a philosophy of mathematics." As Heath amply demonstrates, Plato understood the world *more mathematico*, and for that reason alone the Theraists' interpretation seems outrageously idiosyncratic.
6. R. W. Hutchinson, *Prehistoric Crete* (Baltimore, 1962), p. 23; P. Vidal-Naquet, "Athènes et l'Atlantide," *Revue des Études Grecques* 77 (1964), 425.
7. J. M. Cook, review of J. V. Luce, *The End of Atlantis, Classical Review* 20 (1970), 224–25.
8. For a thorough explication of this principle of contemporary myth theory, not limited to Structuralists like Claude Lévi-Strauss and Edmund Leach, see P. Munz, *When the Golden Bough Breaks* (London, 1973).
9. G. S. Kirk, *Myth: Its Meaning and Functions in Ancient and Other Cultures* (Berkeley, Calif., 1971), pp. 223–26 (*Sather Classical Lectures* 40) and *The Nature of Greek Myths* (Baltimore, 1975), pp. 254–75; T. B. L. Webster, *From Mycenae to Homer*² (London, 1964), pp. 64–90; C. Gordon, *The Common Background of Greek and Hebrew Civilizations* (New York, 1965), *Ugarit and Minoan Crete* (New York, 1966), and *Homer and the Bible* (Ventnor, N.J., 1967).

10. M. L. West (ed.), *Hesiod's Theogony* (Oxford, 1966), pp. 18–30; N. O. Brown, *Hesiod: Theogony, Introduction and Translation* (New York, 1953), pp. 36–46; P. Walcot, *Hesiod and the Near East* (Cardiff, 1966).
11. (Berkeley, Calif., 1959), subtitled "A Study of the Delphic Myth and Its Origins."
12. Kirk (above, note 9, *Greek Myths*), pp. 254–75, includes all these examples in his chapter entitled "The Influence of Western Asia on Greek Myths."
13. *Ancient Near Eastern Literature: A Bibliography of One Thousand Items on the Cuneiform Literatures of the Ancient World* (Ann Arbor, Mich., 1969), Part 5, "Greek-Near Eastern Contacts and Interrelations," pp. 105–13 (items 908–1002).
14. Luce (above, note 4), pp. 148–50; C. Picard, "La Légende d'Oullikoumi et des 'géants-montagnes': de la mythologie hourrite à la gigantomachie grecque," *Revue Archéologique* (1963), 99–101, especially p. 101, note 2.
15. J. Fontenrose, "Philemon, Lot, and Lycaon," *University of California Publications in Classical Philology* 13 (1945), 93–119, confirmed by Emil Kraeling, "Xisouthros, Deucalion, and the Flood Traditions," *Journal of the American Oriental Society* 67 (1947), 177–83 and by Kirk (above, note 9, *Greek Myths*), pp. 116–17, 261–64.
16. For the very real differences in religious ethos and literary formulation between the Old Testament version and its Mesopotamian models, see A. Heidel, *The Gilgamesh Epic and Old Testament Parallels*[2] (Chicago, 1949), pp. 224–69. But see also E. A. Speiser, *The Anchor Bible: Genesis* (Garden City, New York, 1964), pp. 47–57, especially p. 55, where the author notes that "so much correspondence in over-all content is inescapable proof of basic interrelationship."

    The best introduction for the general reader on this issue, though somewhat dated, is A. Parrot, *The Flood and Noah's Ark* (London, 1955).
17. Kirk (above, note 9, *Greek Myths*), p. 263; (above, note 9, *Myth: Its Meaning*), pp. 116–17.
18. Kirk (above, note 9, *Greek Myths*), p. 263.
19. Kirk (above, note 9, *Greek Myths*), pp. 274–75.
20. Kirk (above, note 9, *Greek Myths*), pp. 261–62.
21. See, for example, Galanopoulos and Bacon (above, note 5), pp.

73–74, 121; also A. G. Galanopoulos, "On the Origins of the Deluge of Deukalion and the Myth of Atlantis," *Athenais Archaiologike Hetaireia* 3 (1960), 226–31. Luce (above, note 4), pp. 145–47, who misconceives the origin of the Deucalion legend (it is clearly not Boeotian), resorts to a series of very obscure inundation myths.

22. On the Empedoclean origin of this Platonic version of the cyclical cosmology, see Vidal-Naquet (above, note 6), p. 433, note 69. For Plato's adaptation of Empedoclean theories throughout *Timaeus,* see F. Solmsen, "Tissues and the Soul," *Philosophical Review* 59 (1950), 455–59.
23. J. A. Stewart, *The Myths of Plato* (London, 1905), p. 192.
24. Kirk (above, note 9, *Greek Myths*), pp. 263–68.
25. My interpretation has been anticipated by E. Voegelin, *Order and History,* volume 3, *Plato and Aristotle* (Baton Rouge, La., 1957), pp. 174–78 and by C. Froidefond, *Le mirage égyptien dans la littérature grecque d'Homère à Aristote* (Aix-en-Provence, 1971), pp. 285–90.
26. *Timaeus* 22a; see also *Critias* 112a for another specific allusion to it. Plato's speaker, the Athenian Stranger, in *Laws,* Book 3, refers to this same cyclical pattern of history being exemplified by "*one* of the many catastrophes—namely that which occurred once upon a time through the deluge" (677a).
27. Stewart (above, note 23), pp. 417–18.
28. Kirk (above, note 9, *Greek Myths*), pp. 270–72; Webster (above, note 9), p. 86 and notes 3 and 4.
29. W. Jaeger, *The Theology of the Early Greek Philosophers* (Oxford, 1947), p. 176.
30. Jaeger (above, note 29), p. 184.
31. De Vries (above, note 2), p. 28.
32. For this see *Republic* 2.379 and L. Edelstein, "The Function of the Myth in Plato's Philosophy," *Journal of the History of Ideas* 10 (1949), pp. 465, 479.
33. Edelstein (above, note 32), pp. 472–73.
34. Edelstein (above, note 32), pp. 464–65.
35. Luce (above, note 4), pp. 44–56 (especially p. 53) and p. 214, note 26.
36. Ferguson (above, note 2), p. 105.
37. For an introduction to the history of this myth, see Kirk (above, note 9, *Greek Myths*), index entry "Golden Age"; W. K. C.

Guthrie, *In the Beginning* (Ithaca, N.Y., 1957), pp. 63–79; S. N. Kramer, *History Begins at Sumer* (Garden City, N.Y., 1959), pp. 222–25.

38. For the close relationship between the mythical Golden Age and later utopian speculation, see Ferguson (above, note 2) and A. O. Lovejoy and G. Boas, *A Documentary History of Primitivism and Related Ideas in Antiquity* (Baltimore, 1935), which is a very full account of the sources.
39. Stewart (above, note 23), pp. 179–207; Ferguson (above, note 2), pp. 72–73.
40. The connection is recognized by Voegelin (above, note 25), p. 171, and by A. E. Taylor, *A Commentary on Plato's Timaeus* (Oxford, 1928), p. 13.
41. See Ferguson's chapter on Plato (above, note 2), pp. 61–79, for *Critias* in the context of other Platonic utopian speculations.
42. *Critias* 109b; see also Homer, *Iliad* 15.187–93. For an account of this Greek myth, see F. Solmsen, *Hesiod and Aeschylus* (Ithaca, N.Y., 1949), pp. 5–14 (*Cornell Studies in Classical Philology* 30).
43. *Critias* 109d. For this Greek myth, most popular locally at Athens, see Guthrie (above, note 37), pp. 23–24.
44. See Kirk (above, note 9, *Myth: Its Meaning*), pp. 194–96, 226–32; Ferguson (above, note 2), pp. 72, 74.
45. See Lovejoy and Boas (above, note 38), index entries "Commerce," "Foreign Trade," and "Navigation" and especially pp. 47 and 58, note 74. On page 165 the authors identify the exclusion of commerce in *Republic* as a sign of Plato's "primitivism."
46. *Odyssey* 7.84–132. For Phaeacia as a "source" for Atlantis, see Vidal-Naquet (above, note 6), p. 426.
47. Luce (above, note 4), pp. 171–72.
48. For Phaeacia in the *Odyssey* as a variant of the Golden Age, see Kirk (above, note 9, *Myth: Its Meaning*), pp. 165–69; Ferguson (above, note 2), pp. 13–15. See also M. I. Finley, *The World of Odysseus*[2] (New York, 1965), pp. 105–107.
49. Ferguson (above, note 2), pp. 105, 122–29.
50. De Camp (above, note 1), p. 247.

Atlantis and the Minoan Thalassocracy

1. J. V. Luce, *The End of Atlantis* (U.S.A. title *Lost Atlantis*) (London and New York, 1969), pp. 176–206.

2. Aristotle's view is implied in two passages of Strabo (2.102; 13.598).
3. The fullest survey, with bibliography, of the problem of the identity of Keftiu is J. Vercoutter, *L'Égypte et le monde égéen préhellénique* (Cairo, 1956), who argues that Keftiu is Minoan Crete. So too, more recently, F. Schachermeyr, "Das Keftiu-Problem," *Jahreshefte des Österreichischen Archäologischen Instituts* 45 (1960), 44ff. For Keftiu in Cilicia, see G. Wainwright, "Asiatic Keftiu," *American Journal of Archaeology* 56 (1952), 196–212; A. Furumark, "The Settlement at Ialysos and Aegean History," *Acta Instituti Romani Regni Sueciae* 6 (1950), 243–44. For Keftiu on the coast of Syria, C. Schaeffer, *Ugaritica* (Paris, 1939–62), vol. 1, pp. 34–37; H. Christophe, "Notes geographiques à propos des campagnes de Thutmosis III," *Revue d'Égyptologie* 60 (1951), 89–114. For the Theban tombs, B. Porter and R. Moss, *Topographical Bibliography I²*, *Theban Necropolis I*. A recently discovered text of Amenhotep III may cast further light on the problem; see also E. Edel, *Die Ortsnamenlist aus dem Totentempel Amenophis III* (Bonn, 1966), pp. 33–60; P. Faure, "Toponymes créto-mycéniens dans une liste d'Aménophis III," *Kadmos* 7 (1968), 138–49.
4. These texts can be found in English translation in J. Pritchard, *Ancient Near Eastern Texts Relating to the Old Testament*[3] (Princeton, 1969), pp. 242–43, 374, 441. They, along with other literary references to Keftiu, are discussed by Vercoutter (above, note 3), pp. 38–123.
5. See the works cited above, note 3.
6. For Solon's visit to Egypt, see Herodotus 1.30; 2.177. Aristotle, *Constitution of Athens* 11. Plutarch, *Life of Solon* 26; 31–32; *Moralia* 146E; 354E. Diodorus of Sicily 1.69; 1.96–98. No mention of Saïs occurs in the only extant fragment of Solon referring to Egypt (Plutarch, *Solon* 26). Plutarch's remarks here strongly suggest that Solon's own works contained nothing pertaining to Atlantis.
7. J. Oliver, *The Civilizing Power* in *Transactions of the American Philosophical Society*, New Series 58, part 1 (1968), p. 12.
8. The comment of the scholiast on the opening lines of the *Republic* to the effect that the robe woven for the Lesser Panathenaea was embroidered with figures of the Athenians defeating the Atlanteans has been shown conclusively to be the result of the commentator's misunderstanding a metaphor that Proclus uses (*Commentary on Plato's Timaeus* 26F).
9. B. Jowett, *The Dialogues of Plato*[3] (Oxford, 1892), pp. 429–33.

10. The classic exposition of this view remains M. Nilsson, *The Mycenaean Origin of Greek Mythology* (Berkeley, 1932).
11. A. Evans, *The Palace of Minos* (London, 1921), vol. 1, p. 1.
12. For surveys of the archaeological material, see H. Kantor, *The Aegean and the Near East in the Second Millennium* B.C. (Bloomington, Ind., 1948); R. W. Hutchinson, *Prehistoric Crete* (Baltimore, 1962), pp. 91–122; G. Huxley, *Crete and the Luwians* (Oxford, 1961), pp. 1–7; E. Vermeule, *Greece in the Bronze Age* (Chicago, 1964), pp. 112–55; Luce (above, note 1), pp. 106–44.
13. Pindar, *Paean* 4.30. Bacchylides, *Odes* 1.112.
14. J. D. S. Pendlebury, *The Archaeology of Crete* (London, 1939), pp. 285–89. Quotation, pp. 286–87.
15. Evans (for example, *Palace of Minos*, vol. 1, pp. 24–25) was the great proponent of this view, which continues to enjoy wide acceptance. But C. Starr, "The Myth of the Minoan Thalassocracy," *Historia* 3 (1954–55), 282–91, raised a number of cogent arguments against the acceptance of a Minoan sea empire. With the exception of R. Buck, "The Minoan Thalassocracy Re-examined," *Historia* 11 (1962), 129–37, his arguments have tended to be dismissed rather than refuted by proponents of Cretan imperial power. For a more recent criticism of the notion of a Minoan thalassocracy, see P. Faure, *La vie quotidienne en Crete au temps de Minos (1500 av. J.-C.)* (Paris, 1973), pp. 256–61.
16. The quotation is taken from Frost's article in the London *Times*, February 19, 1909. He returned to the problem in a second study, "The *Critias* and Minoan Crete," *Journal of Hellenic Studies* 33 (1913), 189–206.
17. For discussion of the eruption of Thera and its possible implications for Aegean prehistory see, in addition to the seminal essays by Marinatos in *Antiquity* 13 (1939), 425–39 and in *Kretika Chronika* 2 (1950), 195–213, A. G. Galanopoulos and E. Bacon, *Atlantis: The Truth Behind the Legend* (London, 1969); Luce (above, note 1), pp. 57–206; D. L. Page, *The Santorini Volcano and the Destruction of Minoan Crete* (London, 1970); D. Ninkovich and B. Heezen, "Santorini Tephra," *Colston* [Research Society] *Papers* 17 (1965), 413-53; M. A. Edey, *Lost World of the Aegean* (New York, 1975); S. Hood, "The International Scientific Congress on the Volcano of Thera, 15th–23rd September 1969," *Kadmos* 9 (1970), 98–106; D. B. Vitaliano and C. Vitaliano, "Plinian Eruptions, Earthquakes, and Santorini—A Review," *Acta of the 1st International Congress on the Volcano of Thera, Greece, 1969*

(Athens, 1971), pp. 81–108; D. B. Vitaliano, *Legends of the Earth: Their Geologic Origins* (Bloomington, Ind., 1973); C. Vitaliano and D. Vitaliano, "Volcanic Tephra on Crete," *American Journal of Archaeology* 78 (1974), 19–24; N. Platon, *Zakros: The Discovery of a Lost Palace of Ancient Crete* (New York, 1971), pp. 303–20; R. Carpenter, *Discontinuity in Greek Civilization* (Cambridge, 1966), pp. 27–33.

18. A sensible general survey is provided by Hutchinson (above, note 12), pp. 105–15.
19. S. Marinatos, "La marine créto-mycénienne," *Bulletin de Correspondance Hellénique*" 57 (1933), 170–235, remains the best general study. More recent surveys include Hutchinson (above, note 12), pp. 91–105; L. Casson, *Ships and Seamanship in the Ancient World* (Princeton, 1971), pp. 31ff; Faure (above, note 15), pp. 230–39 with good bibliography and p. 386, note 1; and D. Gray, *Seewesen* (=*Archaeologia Homerica* I, G [Göttingen, 1974]), pp. 33–57, with full bibliographical notes.
20. The standard study of the Egyptian navy in this period is T. Säve-Soderbergh, *The Navy of the Eighteenth Egyptian Dynasty* (Uppsala, 1946). See further H. Biess, *Rekonstruktion ägyptischer Schiffe des neuen Reiches und Terminologie der Schiffsteile* (Diss. Göttingen, 1963); and, briefly, Gray (above, note 19), pp. 47ff.; and Casson (above, note 19), pp. 22ff.
21. This has been pointed out by Starr (above, note 15), pp. 282–91, whose discussion is closely followed in the text. In his criticism of Starr, Buck (above, note 15), pp. 129–37, misses the point of Starr's arguments drawn from comparative naval history.
22. The fresco portraying ships, discovered at Akrotiri on Thera in 1972, is a major new addition to our knowledge of seafaring in the Bronze Age Aegean. However, to the unbiased, it offers no evidence for a Minoan thalassocracy; it is by no means clear that the eight large vessels are warships. Certainly any evidence of military preparation is absent from the scene. Other questions remain: Is the scene necessarily an attempt to picture contemporary life on Crete? The griffin and the subtropical landscape are significant in this context. Is a religious interpretation, a journey to the underworld, out of the question? Is a ship fresco found in Minoanized Thera any surer evidence for Cretan sea power than, for example, a warship on a pyxis from Hellenized Caere is evidence for a Corinthian or Ionian thalassocracy in the seventh-century Mediterranean? For a brief general treatment of the fresco, see S.

Marinatos in *Athens Annals of Archaeology* 6 (1973), 289ff.; and for discussion of the ships see Marinatos' contribution to Gray (above, note 19), pp. 141–52.

23. A convenient translation of the official account of the battle with the Peoples of the Sea can be found in J. Pritchard, *Ancient Near Eastern Texts Relating to the Old Testament*[3] (Princeton, 1969), pp. 262–63.
24. The fullest treatment of Minoa as a place name is M. Faust, "Die ägäische Ortsname Mino(i)a," *Zeitschrift für Vergleichende Sprachforschung* 83 (1969), 88–107.
25. Pausanias, *Description of Greece* 3.23.1 (Laconia). Ptolemy, *Guide to Geography* 3.16.
26. On the location of the various Minoas, there is little to be added to the astute observations of C. Bursian, *Geographie von Griechenland* (Leipzig, 1868–72), vol. 1, pp. 371, 378ff.; vol. 2, pp. 138, 482, 484, 513ff., 535, 544, 574. On the excavation: E. De Miro, "Heraclea Minoa," *Notizie Degli Scavi di Antichità*, series 8, vol. 12 (1958), 232–87.
27. The ancient world knew thirty-three places named Apollonia. See Pauly-Wissowa, *Realenzyklopädie der classischen Altertumswissenschaft*, vol. 3, cols. 111–17. Crete had two Apollonias, as well as two Minoas.
28. Pausanias, *Description of Greece* 1.39.5; 1.44.3; 1.19.4. Apollodorus, *Library* 3.15.
29. See Starr (above, note 15), p. 288; J. W. Graham, *The Palaces of Crete* (Princeton, 1962), p. 14; and much earlier W. Ridgeway, "Minos the Destroyer rather than the Creator of the So-called 'Minoan' Culture of Cnossus," *Proceedings of the British Academy* 4 (1909–10), 97–129.
30. Evans (above, note 11), vol. 4, pp. 944–46.
31. See D. Page, *History and the Homeric Iliad* (Berkeley, Calif., 1963), pp. 118–77; R. Hope Simpson and J. Lazenby, *The Catalogue of Ships in Homer's Iliad* (Oxford, 1970), especially pp. 153–71.
32. L. R. Palmer, *Mycenaeans and Minoans* (New York, 1963), pp. 156–256; Graham (above, note 29), pp. 12–16. The question, critical to the problem of the Catalogue of Ships, receives an extremely summary treatment from Hope Simpson and Lazenby (above, note 31), p. 111.
33. Hutchinson (above, note 12), p. 305.
34. Graham (above, note 29), p. 14.

35. Hesiod, *The Catalogue of Women* 74: "The most kingly of mortal kings ruled over very many people dwelling round about, holding the scepter of Zeus, with which he ruled over the many."
36. M. Ventris and J. Chadwick, *Documents in Mycenaean Greek*[2] (Cambridge, 1973), p. 310.
37. Plutarch, *Greek Questions* 45. 302A. See W. R. Halliday, *The Greek Questions of Plutarch* (Oxford, 1928), pp. 185ff. M. Mayer, "Mykenische Beiträge," *Jahrbuch des Deutschen Archäologischen Instituts* 7 (1892), 191, suggested that *labyrinthos* signified "Place of the Double Axe," and it is a view which has enjoyed wide acceptance. See the bibliography in H. Fisk, *Griechisches etymologisches Wörterbuch* (Heidelberg, 1970), vol. 2, p. 67.
38. L. Deroy, "La valeur du suffixe préhellénique -nth- d'après quelques noms grecs en -nthos," *Glotta* 35 (1957), 173–76. See also A. van Windenkens, *Le pélasgique* (Louvain, 1962), pp. 72–76 and C. Gallavotti, "Labyrinthos," *La Parola del Passato* 12 (1957), 161–76.
39. This is also suggested by R. Meiggs in his brief but perceptive historical analysis of Minoan Crete in J. Bury and R. Meiggs, *History of Greece*[4] (New York, 1975), p. 14.
40. Herodotus 7.169–70. Ephorus quoted by Theon, *Progymnasmata* 16 (=F. Jacoby, *Die Fragmente der griechischen Historiker* [Berlin-Leiden, 1923–   ], No. 70, fragment 57, p. 261). Apollodorus, *Library* 2.6.3. Callimachus 2.118. Strabo 6.2.6. Diodorus 4.79. Ovid, *Art of Love* 2.21ff. *Metamorphoses* 8.183;290.
41. This is pointed out by P. Freidländer, *Platon*[3] (Berlin, 1964), vol. 1, pp. 326–33. For Sicilian influence, see, for example, C. Ritter, *Platon: Sein Leben, seine Schriften, seine Lehre* (Munich, 1923), vol. 2, p. 865.

Atlantis From the Geologic Point of View

1. D. B. Vitaliano, *Legends of the Earth: Their Geologic Origins* (Bloomington, Ind., 1973), pp. 3–4.
2. J. G. Frazer, *Folklore in the Old Testament* (London, 1919), vol. 1, chap. 4, "The Great Flood," pp. 104–361.
3. Ignatius Donnelly, *Atlantis: The Antediluvian World* (New York, 1882).
4. Donnelly cited Santorini as an example of a catastrophically destroyed island. The collapsed part of Santorini is about 83 square

kilometers (about 30 square miles) in area. (Krakatoa, of course, had not yet erupted and collapsed when his book was written.)

5. The earth has a concentrically layered structure. The outer layer is called the *crust*. Under the continents the crust consists of a layer of material which has the properties of basaltic rock, overlain by a layer of granitic material. Under the ocean basins the granitic layer is absent. The crust is only a thin outer skin, ranging in thickness from about 5 kilometers (3 miles) under the oceans to 50 kilometers (30 miles) or so in high mountain areas. The *mantle* beneath it is 1,800 miles thick; its upper part together with the crust constitutes the lithosphere. The *core* of the earth, 2,150 miles in diameter, consists of a solid inner core having the properties of a nickel-iron alloy, surrounded by an outer core which behaves as a liquid (in that its molecules have no fixed structural arrangement) toward the passage of earthquake vibrations.
6. See above, note 5. An excellent popular description of the "plate tectonics" theory and its development can be found in a series of articles in *The New Yorker* entitled "Explorer" (a profile of Maurice Ewing), which appeared in the issues of November 4, 11, and 18, 1974. A more scientific presentation of the details is found in H. Takeuchi, S. Uyeda, and H. Kanamori, *Debate about the Earth* (San Francisco, 1967).
7. R. Claiborne, *The First Americans* (New York, 1973), pp. 38–39 (*Time-Life Emergence of Man Series*).
8. L. Spence, *The Problem of Atlantis* (New York, 1925).
9. This argument is also cited in the Modern Revised Edition of Donnelly's book (New York, 1949).
10. P. Termier, "Atlantis," *Annual Report of the Smithsonian Institution* (1915), 219–34.
11. J. G. Moore, "Petrology of Deep-Sea Basalt near Hawaii," *American Journal of Science* 263 (1965), 40–52.
12. C. Berlitz, *The Mystery of Atlantis* (New York, 1969), pp. 196–98.
13. L. S. de Camp, *Lost Continents* (New York, 1954; Dover ed., 1970), pp. 314–18.
14. L. S. Berg, "Atlantida i Egeida," *Priroda* 4 (1928), 383-88.
15. W. Harrison, "Atlantis Undiscovered—Bimini, Bahamas," *Nature* 230 (1971), 287–89.
16. A. G. Galanopoulos, "On the Origin of the Deluge of Deukalion and the Myth of Atlantis," *Athenais Archaiologike Hetaireia* 3 (1960), 226–31.

17. K. T. Frost, "The *Critias* and Minoan Crete," *Journal of Hellenic Studies* 33 (1913), 189–206.
18. A. G. Galanopoulos and E. Bacon, *Atlantis: The Truth behind the Legend* (London, 1969).
19. The whole group of islands, consisting of the three remnants of the original island (Thera, Therasia, and tiny Aspronisi) plus Palea and Nea Kameni in the middle of the bay, formed since the Bronze Age eruption, is known to geologists as the Santorini volcano. The name Thera, which is the official governmental name for the whole group as well as the name of its largest island, seems to be preferred by archaeologists and classical scholars. In this work, I use Santorini to designate the whole group and Thera to designate the one island in that group.
20. Vitaliano (above, note 1), pp. 237–38.
21. D. Ninkovich and B. Heezen, "Santorini Tephra," *Colston* [Research Society] *Papers* 17 (1965), 413–53.
22. *Magma* is molten rock material generated within the earth and capable of being intruded or extruded. It may contain solid substances, such as crystals and rock fragments, and gases. Lava is magma which flows out on the earth's surface.
23. They are also popularly called "tidal waves," but that is quite erroneous, inasmuch as they have nothing whatever to do with the tides.
24. Vitaliano (above, note 1), p. 150.
25. Ninkovich and Heezen (above, note 21), p. 443.
26. R. F. Griggs, *The Valley of Ten Thousand Smokes* (Washington, 1922), p. 25.
27. Vitaliano (above, note 1), pp. 17–18.
28. Griggs (above, note 26), pp. 46–47.
29. H. Reck, *Santorin: Der Werdegang eines Inselvulkans und sein Ausbruch 1925–28* (Berlin, 1936), vol. 1.
30. B. Heezen, "A Time Clock for History," *Saturday Review*, December 6, 1969, 64–72. S. Hood, "The International Scientific Congress on the Volcano of Thera, 15th–23rd September 1969," *Kadmos* 9 (1970), 98–106.
31. J. G. Moore, "Base Surge in Recent Volcanic Eruptions," *Bulletin Volcanologique* 30 (1967), 40–52.
32. S. Marinatos, "Thera: Key to the Riddle of Minos," *National Geographic* 141 (May, 1972), 40–52.
33. Hood (above, note 30), p. 104.

34. C. Doumas, "The Minoan Eruption of the Santorini Volcano," *Antiquity* 48 (1974), 110–15.
35. D. B. Vitaliano and C. Vitaliano, "Plinian Eruptions, Earthquakes, and Santorin–A Review," *Acta of the 1st International Scientific Congress on the Volcano of Thera, Greece, 1969* (Athens, 1971), pp. 88–108.
36. Hood (above, note 30), pp. 103–104.
37. J. V. Luce, "Thera and the Devastation of Minoan Crete: A New Interpretation of the Evidence," *American Journal of Archaeology* 80 (1976), 9–16.
38. C. and D. Vitaliano, "Volcanic Tephra on Crete," *American Journal of Archaeology* 78 (1974), 19–24.
39. Particles of ash from the Bronze Age eruption of Santorini have been identified in samples collected from Late Minoan I levels at Phylakopi on Melos in 1974. It is hoped that the results of the 1975 excavations will make it possible to date these levels more closely, that is, Late Minoan I A or Late Minoan I B equivalents.
40. N. Platon, "La destruction volcanique du centre palatial de Zakros," *Acta of the 1st International Scientific Congress on the Volcano of Thera, Greece, 1969* (Athens, 1971), p. 399; also *Zakros: The Discovery of a Lost Palace of Ancient Crete* (New York, 1971), p. 291.
41. Vitaliano and Vitaliano (above, note 35), p. 98.
42. Vitaliano (above, note 1), pp. 209–17.

Glacial Fluctuations, Sea-level Changes, and Catastrophic Floods

1. R. F. Flint, *Glacial and Quaternary Geology* (New York, 1971), chapter 12.
2. H. E. Wright, Jr., "Late Quaternary Vegetational History of North America," in K. K. Turekian, ed., *Late Cenozoic Glacial Ages* (New Haven, Conn., 1971), pp. 425–64.
3. A. L. Bloom, "Glacial-Eustatic and Isostatic Controls of Sea Level since the Last Glaciation," in K. K. Turekian, ed. (above, note 2), pp. 355–79.
4. C. Emiliani, S. Gartner, B. Lidz, K. Eldridge, D. K. Elvey, T. C. Huang, J. J. Stipp, and M. F. Swanson, "Paleoclimatological Analysis of Late Quaternary Cores from the Northeastern Gulf of Mexico," *Science* 189 (1975), 1083–88.
5. Bloom (above, note 3).

6. D. M. Mickelson and E. B. Evenson, "Pre-Twocreekan Age of the Type Valders Till, Wisconsin," *Geology* 3 (1975), 587–90.
7. H. E. Wright, Jr., "Tunnel Valleys, Glacial Surge, and Subglacial Hydrology of the Superior Lobe, Minnesota," *Geological Society of America Memoir* 136 (1973), 251–76.
8. F. G. Driscoll, *Formation and Wastage of Neoglacial Surge Moraines of the Klutlan Glacier, Yukon Territory* (Minneapolis, Minn., 1976) (University of Minnesota Dissertation).
9. H. E. Wright, Jr., "Quaternary History of Minnesota," in P. K. Sims and G. B. Morey, eds., *Geology of Minnesota* (Minneapolis, 1972), pp. 515–48.
10. J. P. Kennett and N. J. Shackelton, "Laurentide Ice Sheet Meltwater Recorded in Gulf of Mexico Deep-Sea Cores," *Science* 188 (1975), 147–50.

Further Reading

The following list is meant to supplement the essays and is by no means complete. The many accounts that have appeared in pulp paperback form are not included, simply because most of them have little reliable information to offer. An asterisk (*) indicates those books or articles in each section that give a good overview of the particular subject, either individually or together.

I. *Surveys of Atlantis Literature and Earlier Theories*

1. J. Bramwell, *Lost Atlantis* (London, 1937).
2. H. Cherniss, "Plato 1950–57," *Lustrum* 4 (1959), 79–83.

*3. L. S. de Camp, *Lost Continents: The Atlantis Theme in History and Literature* (New York, 1954; Dover ed., 1970).

*4. J. Gattefossé and C. Roux, *Bibliographie de l'Atlantide et des questions connexes* (Cannes, 1926).

*5. T. H. Martin, *Études sur le Timée de Platon* (Paris, 1841), vol. 1, pp. 257–333.

6. J. Rexine, "Atlantis: Fact or Fantasy," *Classical Bulletin* 51 (1974–75), 49–53.
7. D. B. Vitaliano, "Atlantis: A Review Essay," *Journal of the Folklore Institute* 8 (1971), 68–76.

See also 8, 13, 14, 73, 80.

II. *Plato's Account of Atlantis in the* Timaeus *and* Critias

8. W. Brandenstein, *Grösse und Untergang eines geheimnisvolle Inselreiches* (Vienna, 1951).

9. R. S. Brumbaugh, "A Note on the Numbers in Plato's *Critias*," *Classical Philology* 43 (1948), 40–42.
10. C. Corbato, "In margine alla questione atlantidea. Platone e Cartagine," *Archeologia Classica* 5 (1953), 232–37.
*11. L. Edelstein, "The Function of Myth in Plato's Philosophy," *Journal of the History of Ideas* 10 (1949), 463–81.
12. P. Frutiger, *Les mythes de Platon* (Paris, 1930).
13. R. Hackforth, "The Story of Atlantis: Its Purpose and Moral," *Classical Review* 58 (1944), 7–9.
14. W. A. Heidel, "A Suggestion Concerning Plato's Atlantis," *Proceedings of the American Academy of Arts and Sciences* 68 (1932–33), 189–228.
15. E. D. Phillips, "Historical Elements in the Myth of Atlantis," *Euphrosyne* 2 (1968), 3–38.
16. Proclus, *Commentary on Plato's Timaeus,* ed. Diehl (Leipzig, 1903).
17. ———, *Commentaire sur le Timée*, ed. A. J. Festugière (Paris, 1966–67).
18. T. G. Rosenmeyer, "The Numbers in Plato's Critias: A Reply," *Classical Philology* 44 (1949), 117–20.
19. ———, "Plato's Atlantis Myth: *Timaeus* or *Critias,*" *Phoenix* 10 (1956), 163–72.
*20. J. A. Stewart, *The Myths of Plato* (London, 1905).
21. A. E. Taylor, *A Commentary on Plato's Timaeus* (Oxford, 1928), pp. 49–57.
*22. P. Vidal-Naquet, "Athènes et l'Atlantide," *Revue des Études Grecques* 77 (1964), 420–44.
23. R. Weil, *L'archéologie de Platon* (Paris, 1959).

See also 2, 3, 41, 53, 56, 80.

III. *Atlantis and Mythology*

24. S. G. F. Brandon, *Creation Legends of the Ancient Near East* (London, 1963).
25. R. Chase, *Quest for Myth* (Baton Rouge, La., 1949).
26. P. Cohen, "Theories of Myth," *Man* n.s. 4 (1969), 337–53.
27. J. D. Cooke, "Euhemerism: A Medieval Interpretation of Classical Paganism," *Speculum* 2 (1927), 396–410.
28. B. Feldman and R. D. Richardson, *The Rise of Modern Mythology 1680–1860* (Bloomington, Ind., 1972).
*29. J. Ferguson, *Utopias of the Classical World* (Ithaca, N.Y., 1975).

*30. J. Fontenrose, "Philemon, Lot, and Lycaon," *University of California Publications in Classical Philology* 13 (1945), 93–119.
31. J. G. Frazer, *Folklore in the Old Testament* (London, 1919).
32. C. Froidefond, *Le mirage égyptien dans la littérature grecque d'Homère à Aristote* (Aix-en-Provence, 1971).
33. A. G. Galanopoulos, "On the Origin of the Deluge of Deukalion and the Myth of Atlantis," *Athenais Archaiologike Hetaireia* 3 (1960), 226–31.
34. C. Gordon, *The Common Background of Greek and Hebrew Civilizations* (New York, 1965).
35. ———, *Ugarit and Minoan Crete* (New York, 1966).
*36. G. S. Kirk, *Myth: Its Meaning and Functions in Ancient and Other Cultures* (Berkeley, 1971) (*Sather Classical Lectures* 40).
*37. ———, *The Nature of Greek Myths* (Baltimore, 1975).
38. P. Munz, *When the Golden Bough Breaks* (London, 1973).
*39. A Parrot, *The Flood and Noah's Ark* (London, 1955).
40. J. Peradotto, *Classical Mythology: An Annotated Bibliography* (Urbana, Ill., 1973).
*41. E. Voegelin, *Order and History,* volume 3, *Plato and Aristotle* (Baton Rouge, La., 1957), pp. 170–214 ("*Timaeus* and *Critias*").
42. J. de Vries, *Forschungsgeschichte der Mythologie* (Munich, 1961), pp. 28–30 (Euhemerus).
43. T. B. L. Webster, *From Mycenae to Homer*² (London, 1964), pp. 64–90 ("Eastern Poetry and Mycenaean Poetry").

See also 11, 12, 13, 20, 22, 56.

IV. *Crete and the Minoan Eruption on Thera (Santorini)*

A. General on Crete

44. A. Evans, *The Palace of Minos* (London, 1921–1935).
45. P. Faure, *La vie quotidienne en Crete au temps de Minos (1500 av. J.-C.)* (Paris, 1973).
46. J. W. Graham, *The Palaces of Crete* (Princeton, 1962).
*47. R. W. Hutchinson, *Prehistoric Crete* (Baltimore, 1962).
48. J. D. S. Pendlebury, *The Archaeology of Crete* (London, 1939).

B. Thera and Crete

*49. *Acta of the 1st International Scientific Congress on the Volcano of Thera, Greece, 1969* (Athens, 1971).

*50. R. Buck, "The Minoan Thalassocracy Re-examined," *Historia* 11 (1962), 129–37.

51. R. Carpenter, *Discontinuity in Greek Civilization* (Cambridge, 1966), pp. 27–33.

52. C. Doumas, "The Minoan Eruption of the Santorini Volcano," *Antiquity* 48 (1974), 110–15.

*53. K. T. Frost, "The *Critias* and Minoan Crete," *Journal of Hellenic Studies* 33 (1913), 189–206.

54. A. G. Galanopoulos and E. Bacon, *Atlantis: The Truth Behind the Legend* (London, 1969).

55. S. Hood, "The International Scientific Congress on the Volcano of Thera, 15th–23rd September, 1969," *Kadmos* 9 (1970), 98–106.

*56. J. V. Luce, *The End of Atlantis* (U.S.A. title *Lost Atlantis*) (London and New York, 1969).

*57. ———, "Thera and the Devastation of Minoan Crete: A New Interpretation of the Evidence," *American Journal of Archaeology* 80 (1976), 9–16.

58. Sp.Marinatos, "The Volcanic Destruction of Minoan Crete," *Antiquity* 13 (1939), 425–39.

59. ———, *Excavations at Thera I–VI* (Athens, 1968–1974) (*Bibliotheke tes en Athenais Archaiologikes Hetaireias* 64).

60. ———, *Some Words About the Legend of Atlantis*[2] (Athens, 1971).

*61. ———, "Thera: Key to the Riddle of Minos," *National Geographic* 141 (May, 1972), 40–52.

62. J. W. Mavor, *Voyage to Atlantis* (New York, 1969).

63. A. Nicaise, *Thera, l'Atlantide et Krakatoa: Les terres disparues* (Paris, 1885).

*64. D. L. Page, *The Santorini Volcano and the Destruction of Minoan Crete* (London, 1970) (Society for the Promotion of Hellenic Studies, Supplementary Paper No. 12).

*65. N. Platon, *Zakros: The Discovery of a Lost Palace of Ancient Crete* (New York, 1971), pp. 303–20.

66. C. Seltman, "Life in Ancient Crete—II: Atlantis," *History Today* 2 (1952), 332–43.

67. J. W. Sperling, *Thera and Therasia* (Athens 1973) (*Ancient Greek Cities* 22).

*68. C. Starr, "The Myth of the Minoan Thalassocracy," *Historia* 3 (1954–55), 282–91.

*69. D. B. Vitaliano and C. Vitaliano, "Plinian Eruptions, Earthquakes, and Santorin—a Review," *Acta of the First International Congress* *on the Volcano of Thera, Greece, 1969* (Athens, 1971), pp. 81–108.

See also 7, 76, 79, 80.

V. *Atlantis and Geology*

70. J. G. Bennett, "Geo-physics and Human History: New Light on Plato's Atlantis," *Systematics* 1 (1963), 127–56.
71. C. Emiliani *et al.*, "Paleoclimatological Analysis of Late Quaternary Cores from the Northeastern Gulf of Mexico," *Science* 189 (1975), 1083–88.
72. L. D. Leet, *The Causes of Catastrophe* (New York, 1948), pp. 215, 219–20.
73. W. D. Matthew, "Plato's Atlantis in Palaeogeography," *Proceedings of the National Academy of Sciences* 6 (1920), 17–18.
74. J. G. Moore, "Petrology of Deep-Sea Basalt Near Hawaii," *American Journal of Science* 263 (1965), 40–52.
75. ———, "Base Surge in Recent Volcanic Eruptions," *Bulletin Volcanologique* 30 (1967), 40–52.
*76. D. Ninkovich and B. Heezen, "Santorini Tephra," *Colston* [Research Society] *Papers* 17 (1965), 413–53.
*77. C. Schuchert, "Atlantis and the Permanency of the North Atlantic Ocean Bottom," *Proceedings of the National Academy of Sciences* 3 (1917), 65–72.
78. P. Termier, "Atlantis," *Annual Report of the Smithsonian Institution* (1915), 219–34.
*79. C. and D. Vitaliano, "Volcanic Tephra on Crete," *American Journal of Archaeology* 78 (1974), 19–24.
*80. D. B. Vitaliano, *Legends of the Earth* (Bloomington, Ind., 1973).
81. H. E. Wright, Jr., "Tunnel Valleys, Glacial Surges, and the Subglacial Hydrology of the Superior Lobe of Minnesota," *Geological Society of America Memoir* 136 (1973), 251–76.

See also 7, 49, 52, 55, 56, 57, 58, 63, 64, 69.

Index